You're Tearing Us Apart

You're Tearing Us Apart

Twenty Ways We Wreck Our Relationships and Strategies to Repair Them

Pat Love, Eva Berlander, and Kathleen McFadden
Illustrated by Anders Berlander

Health Communications, Inc.
Deerfield Beach, Florida

www.hcibooks.com

**Library of Congress Cataloging-in-Publication Data
is available through the Library of Congress**

© 2015 Pat Love, Eva Berlander, and Kathleen McFadden

ISBN-13: 978-07573-1862-7 (Paperback)
ISBN-10: 07573-1862-2 (Paperback)
ISBN-13: 978-07573-1863-4 (ePub)
ISBN-10: 07573-1863-0 (ePub)

Publisher: Health Communications, Inc.
3201 S.W. 15th Street
Deerfield Beach, FL 33442–8190

Cover illustration by Anders Berlander
Cover and interior design by Lawna Patterson Oldfield

Contents

Acknowledgments

I n fifty years of training we've come across many great teachers who whisper from the pages of this book. A comprehensive list would be too difficult to remember and too long to read. At times, however, a teacher comes along who dramatically influences the way you think and must be recognized; Dan Siegel is one of those. His approach to interpersonal neurobiology in general, and the integration of differentiated parts in specific, are fundamental elements of the change process required to keep our relationships stable and satisfying. We appreciate his brilliance and professional generosity.

Steven Stosny's work also is evidenced in the pages that follow. His insights related to core values have helped thousands of individuals and couples regain personal integrity and turn problems into progress.

Living with an author requires an expected amount of patience and support, but when there are three authors and two continents involved, even more is entailed. Sven, Anders, and Nikolas Berlander can attest to this. While supporting Eva in her writing they also embraced more than one U.S. invasion in their home for days at a time. On the other side of the Atlantic, Larry, Devin, and Katie had to hold down the fort while Pat and Kathleen worked, but also relished that unique Scandinavian hospitality. Thank you all for being there.

Finally, Christine Belleris didn't shy away from the prospect of two Texans and a Swede writing together with another Swede illustrating it all. She encouraged us, believed in the project, and saw how powerful this innovative book could be. We needed that! Our appreciations go to you, Christine.

Authors' Note:
Why This Book?

The divorce rate hovers around 50 percent in the United States, and 30 percent of those who are still married report living separate lives. Alarmingly, about 60 percent of couples who ultimately divorce come from *low-conflict* marriages that have a great chance of surviving and thriving with minimal change. Many broken relationships not only can be mended, but magnificent.

Few would argue against the fact that life in the twenty-first century is far more complicated. Today's relationships face enormous pressure and time constraints not seen a mere generation ago. One recent study found that couples spend only thirty-five minutes per week in intimate conversation; the rest of the time they rely on electronic contact and sticky notes. Gone are the times when two people sat down each evening and leisurely discussed happenings of the day. Instead, couples are texting, tweeting, and exchanging emotions for emoticons. This fast-paced life calls for fast-paced strategies, and this book is full of them!

For convenience and efficiency each chapter follows a simple, get-to-the-point formula. First, a narrative describes what it's like living with someone who is practicing relationship-threatening behaviors. The original artwork in each chapter illustrates the significance of these behaviors even further. Next, we explain the psychology behind the behavior, followed by a succinct account of why each behavior threatens relationships. Finally, we spell out results-oriented strategies for transformation in menu form, covering a wide range of options for even the most complex issues. These four sections validate the experience of both partners, offer concrete reasons why change is necessary, and then present a selection of actions for moving forward.

One final note of significance: the writing and artwork in this book are inclusive, meaning gender and sexual orientation neutral.

We hope you enjoy this book as much as we have enjoyed the collaborative experience of putting it together!

—*Pat, Eva, Kathleen, and Anders*

Introduction:
You're Tearing Us Apart

C hances are you've heard it takes two people to destroy a relationship, but experience proves otherwise. One person *can* do the deed alone. Trust can be destroyed by one uncovered email account, one criticism too many, or one last drunken argument. Unilateral actions are taken, and many destroy relationships.

Think about it: *You don't make me drink. I don't make you overwork. I didn't create your technology obsession. You didn't make me spend too much.* These are personal choices that destroy trust and intimacy, which are the lifeblood of relationship connection.

But here is the good news: If one person can tear a relationship apart, one person can fix it—and you can fix it in three steps:

Step One: Recognize the part of your behavior that undermines intimacy.

Step Two: Replace harmful behaviors with healthy acts of love.

Step Three: Repeat Steps One and Two!

Transforming a relationship isn't rocket science, and we've made it uncomplicated by using more than fifty years of combined professional experience and scientific study to make the transformation simple, speedy, and satisfying. A shift in one partner's attitude and actions can create a positive ripple effect throughout the relationship and restore intimate connection.

The tried-and-true strategies in this short, user-friendly book help both individuals and couples to identify the types of behaviors that tear couples apart, explain why these behaviors are destructive, and provide alternatives for repair and transformation.

Whether you read this book entirely, or select specific chapters, you can start with a few small changes to make your relationship more rewarding than ever.

1

Your Criticism Is Tearing Us Apart

*If you only knew how hurtful it is when you criticize me.
No matter what I do, nothing ever seems good enough.
Every day I work as hard as I can to contribute to our relationship,
but instead of a welcome smile or a little appreciation, what I get is
your displeasure and ultimately more complaints. Truthfully, when
you are around I have to brace myself because somehow you have the
ability to turn the most positive conversation into a criticism.*

*It's discouraging when other people recognize all the good things I
do, but you—the one I love most and the reason behind everything
I do—can recall only those things I didn't do. I try and try to please
you, never getting a "thank you" or praise for what I do right. As soon
as I do something wrong in your eyes, I hear about it, not just once,
but time and time again. I feel like you never see what I do, only what
I don't do. It's so difficult for me to keep trying when you continually
point out how I have failed.*

*It saddens me that what I do isn't good enough in your eyes. I think
we have a good life full of positives, but what I hear most from you is
negatives. This burden grows heavier the longer we are together.*

The Purpose Behind Criticism

As strange as it sounds, criticism has a positive purpose: it's an
attempt to evoke a change in the relationship. Complaint, comparison, and blame are ways of letting you know something needs
to shift; but even though it is aimed toward a solution, criticism
often becomes the problem.

Partners who criticize aren't fully aware of the impact because, typically, they are trying to communicate a desire for change that they feel will *improve* the relationship. Although their intentions are positive, they don't realize the result is negative. What may be a cry for help still sounds like a criticism. For example, "You don't listen to me," may mean, "I want you to show interest in me by remembering our conversations because that makes me feel close to you and loved by you." Or, "All you ever think about is sex," may mean, "I want to have sex with you and it takes an emotional connection to ignite my desire."

One common point of confusion regarding criticism is how men and women differ in their responses to it. Neither likes it, but if a woman complains to another woman, "The kids are driving me crazy!" most women will move in closer to comfort or console. "I am so sorry. Tell me what's going on." But if a woman complains to a man, "The kids are driving me crazy!" he knows sooner or later it's going to be his fault. Most men are fixers, and so a woman's complaint feels like his failure for not fixing the problem or preventing it from happening in the first place. Interestingly, when a man criticizes another man, it's often in the form of banter or sparring; it even can be a way of helping him improve, for instance, "If you get a better haircut you might get a date!"

Behind every criticism is a desire, but when a desire is delivered and received in a negative manner, the medium is the message and the message is a menace.

The Disconnect from Criticism

Most human beings respond to criticism the very same way: We defend against it. Some people defend by trying harder and apologizing. Others defend by withdrawing, getting angry, or losing hope. When criticized, your psyche switches into a defensive mode, and while this protection is in place, connection with your partner is broken. With repeated criticism you'll eventually associate your partner with pain, not pleasure, leaving you no choice but to tune out and disconnect. If and when this happens, the distance between you will widen at an alarming rate.

Interpersonal neurobiology helps explain why relationship connection is critical to our well-being—not to mention our survival. One of our greatest human strengths is attachment. We can't survive as infants or thrive as adults without contact or connection with others. We need to be understood, cared about, and, from time-to-time, have another individual experience a state of mind similar to our own.

Mirror neurons help explain why human emotions are contagious. These neurons in the brain continually reflect the moods and emotions of people around us, both positive and negative. The good news is mirror neurons provide the basis of learning and enable us to feel empathy. The bad news is mirror neurons, like a sponge, take in and reflect negative emotions and behaviors as well. We simply feel what others feel because our emotional states are contagious. This is why living with a critical person is stressful just like living with a depressed person is depressing—we influence, and are influenced by, each other's emotions.

Criticism comes in all forms: cutting words; sounds, such as a heavy sigh; and bodily expressions like piercing eyes, wrinkled forehead, or threatening body posture. These expressions bounce back and forth between us like a ball in a tennis match and ultimately determine the tenor and outcome of the game.

Continual criticism ultimately can lead to contempt, the single greatest predictor of divorce and separation. Contempt means, "I've made up my mind about you and it's not good." Contempt keeps you from seeing what your partner does right while only seeing what your partner does wrong.

Criticism is stressful for both partners and keeps you both on edge. As long as defenses are up, connection is down. Couples who are disconnected risk growing apart, which is the most commonly cited cause of divorce and separation.

Transforming Criticism

Behind every blame, judgment, complaint, and criticism is a desire, so cut to the chase—go straight to your desire. Ask for what you want in an affirmative way. State your desire positively, measurably, and specifically.

> *"I would love for you to plan one evening a month alone for us where we have no phones or electronics for a three-hour block of time."*

You can transform criticism by stating the underlying desire. Be clever, not critical. You can eliminate the need for criticism altogether by catching your partner in the act of doing something right—even a seemingly mundane thing—and acknowledging it.

> *"It really helped when you unloaded the dishwasher."*
>
> *"Thank you for the wonderful hug you just gave me."*
>
> *"It feels so good when you smile at me and look at me with those soft eyes."*

"Thank you for remembering I had that review at work today because your note of encouragement lifted my spirits."

Your partner is very interested in your desires but cannot hear you when they come in the form of criticism. Stay connected by sending your positive message in a positive package.

Don't forget you can catch a mood, so try infecting your partner with positivity. Remember to differentiate. The only person you can change is yourself, and you alone can promote positive change and help keep the path clear for connection by transforming criticism into desire and appreciation.

2

Your Mood Swings Are Tearing Us Apart

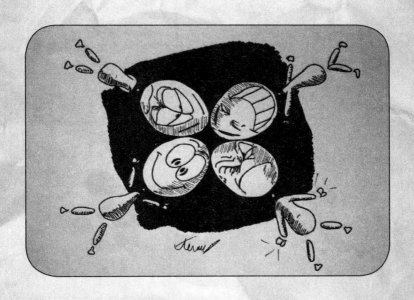

I feel like I'm walking on eggshells. From one moment to the next, I never know what your mood will be like. One minute we're having a good time enjoying the day, then all of a sudden your mood just flips like a light switch!

When that happens there's nothing I can say or do that seems to help. You go to this place in your head that I don't understand and I can't seem to reach you, let alone reason with you. It's like a curtain comes down and you are in a world of your own. Every time I try reaching out, you either get irritated or go silent, inevitably shutting me out and pushing me away. At times it feels like you go so far off the deep end I don't know if you'll ever come back.

Was it something I did? Was it something I said? I've tried to figure out if my actions or words trigger a shift in your mood. I've changed my behavior to try pleasing you. When you ask me to do something, I do it to the best of my ability, but no matter what I do it never seems to have any positive impact on you. I'm constantly on guard and your demands keep getting bigger and more difficult.

Ultimately, I'm afraid you'll make demands so unrealistic and unachievable that any shortcomings will give you permission to leave me forever. I feel hopeless and like a complete failure.

The Purpose Behind Mood Swings

As difficult as it is tiptoeing around a partner in a bad mood, bear in mind that his or her pain is as great as—or even greater than—yours. People in a bad mood lash out in a misguided attempt to feel better. Sometimes it's a cry for help; other times it's a crass effort at an emotional exorcism. Either way, the volatile nature of mood swings causes chaos for both partners in relationships.

Emotions make life enjoyable and enrich many experiences, such as falling in love, sharing a hobby, exploring nature, or mastering a new skill. Emotions also make life miserable and cause great damage when they are inappropriate for the situation: too intense, unstable, always negative, or out of control.

Emotions motivate you to think, feel, and behave in certain ways. While you can't prevent emotions from emerging entirely, you can learn to identify triggers, modify your behavior, and manage your reactivity in constructive ways.

A mood often manifests from feeling a particular emotion for a period of time. There are good moods and bad moods. A bad mood covers everything in a cloud of negativity. A good mood filters everything through a positive light.

Good or bad, moods and emotions affect everything and everyone around us. When moods are unpredictable or swing without forewarning, the resultant instability can tear a relationship apart.

The Disconnect from Mood Swings

Moods are contagious. Thanks to mirror neurons and the nervous system, your brain is designed to pick up on another person's disposition. Sometimes you'll feel a wave of discomfort or energy in the room without realizing you're sharing emotions through non-verbal cues, like facial expression, eye gaze, and body posture. Having a sense of what another person is thinking or feeling enables you to foresee and prepare for a proper response. It's an internal alert system.

Designed for fight-or-flight speed and survival, this alarm system consistently surveys the landscape asking, "Am I safe?" Your body's physical and emotional responses to that question are automatic, but not always *accurate*, because they are altered by your perceptions and past experiences. Oftentimes you must act *despite* your feelings to avoid behaving inappropriately or over-reacting. Without emotional self-regulation, repeat behaviors consistently will produce poor results.

When your partner is unhappy or in distress, it's natural for you to feel distressed as well. The challenge is relating to your partner's pain instead of reeling from it, to manage your own emotional responses to your partner's feelings. Relating to another's pain is a hallmark of compassion, which is the desire to ease suffering. Compassion also promotes protection and provides a positive framework for resolving issues.

Sometimes showing compassion helps; sometimes it doesn't. If you caused your partner's distress, then likely you can fix it. But if your partner's pain is a personal issue, only your partner's own actions will make it better.

Mood swings often unfold into arguments because both partners' emotions escalate beyond effectiveness. Couples often "push each other's buttons" to the point of a big blow-up or silent shutdown. Emotional turmoil takes a toll on relationships, often leaving one or both partners in a state of despair.

Extended bad moods with no apparent cause ultimately will create distance between two people. When a partner's attempts to help repeatedly fail, hopelessness is never far behind and the couple grows farther apart.

Transforming Mood Swings

Most people don't consciously choose a bad mood, but staying in a good mood is easier for some than others. Negative mood swings come from nature, nurture, and negative behaviors. They are hardest on the person in the swing but also difficult for those in the line of fire.

Nature. We are each born with a unique biochemical set point that determines much of how we think and feel. Neurological chemicals (neurotransmitters, hormones) in the body directly affect mood, behavior, decision-making, and ability to manage stress. Lifestyle choices such as diet, exercise, stress, smoking, substance abuse (alcohol, drugs, medication), and environmental exposures also affect biochemistry and can alter the way we feel.

Some people are born with a biochemistry that requires direct measures for maintaining positive feelings and a good attitude. Some people experience a biochemical shift or depletion over time. Advising them to "Cheer up" or "Look on the bright side" doesn't help. It's nearly impossible to have fun or hold a positive thought without the right biochemical balance. When positive thoughts and actions do not lift the mood, it's time for professional help. Fortunately, great help is available. *No one should suffer alone in this day and age.* If you suspect biochemistry is the culprit, start with primary medical care and go from there.

Nurture. Neurological chemicals influence behavior, making some people naturally optimistic and lighthearted, others more serious and pensive. Past experiences and associations also shape your perceptions and significantly influence the way your brain responds. Anytime you have an experience that's important enough to remember, your brain marks it with emotion.

For example, if you were pushed away, blamed, or abandoned by an important person to whom you were emotionally attached, your brain would mark that experience with anxiety—which would put you on high alert for future relationships. Fast-forward to a new romance. After the high of infatuation passes (when your brain is flooded with feel-good chemicals), your brain automatically recalls the emotional marker. But recall often occurs without specific memory or awareness of the past event. All you know is that you feel anxious in this relationship now, and blaming your partner is the brain's way of making sense of your sensations.

Mood swings often erupt from confusing the past with the present. Simply being aware of the confusion can be helpful. Awareness is an important first step toward identifying triggers, differentiating past feelings from present, and ultimately transforming behavior in a constructive way.

When negative moods influence a relationship it helps to delineate between your stuff, my stuff, and our stuff. The person subject to moodiness might let the other partner know how to assist using simple suggestions:

"When I am in a bad mood it helps me when . . ."

"Thank you for . . . When I was feeling down, that really helped."

"You don't have to worry about me or do anything right now.
    I'm just going to take a nap and take care of myself."
"Right now it would help take the stress off if you . . ."

If you are the partner wanting to help, a simple statement like this could create a positive shift:

"Honey, how can I help?"
"What's one thing I could do right now that might help?"

Differentiating past feelings from present isn't always achievable on your own. Left unattended, emotional markers like anxiety can turn into depression. Fortunately, we live in a time when mental health professionals can help alleviate these issues.

Negative behaviors. Negative thoughts cause negative feelings. Negative behaviors cause negative feelings.

Some of us suffer from "stinking thinking" with bad mental habits. Looking on the down side of life does have merit, but looking and living there are two different things. Research shows that even forcing yourself to count your blessings, to grin and have gratitude, *can* help.

Instead of stewing in negativity, practice thought-stopping and start chewing on something positive. Be intentional. Regularly seek opportunities to take in positive instead of following negative inclinations. With repetitive positive experience, you can rewire your brain to regulate negative feelings and create good mental habits. Practice positive thinking every day. Pay attention and reinforce positive moments by staying with the good feeling for ten to twenty-five seconds at a time.

Bad habits can cause bad moods, so can a bad job, bad commute, bad weather, and all-around bad options. When chocolate, caffeine, meditation, exercise, laughing, loving, sex, or a silly movie don't work, then run—don't walk—for help.

Although we each experience varying degrees of positive and negative emotions, individual emotional experiences are unique, biochemically influenced, and shaped by perceptions. For each partner, at times it can bring comfort knowing: *you can't always control what happens to you in life, but you can control how you respond to it.*

3

Your Porn/Chat Room Use Is Tearing Us Apart

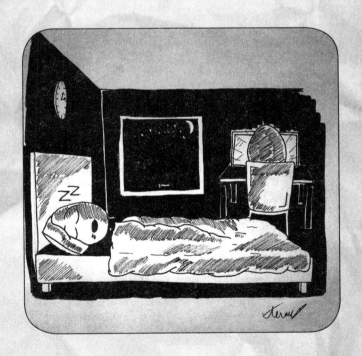

I'm worried about our relationship.

You've changed. You don't feel the same about me and you don't feel the same about us. You are distant, preoccupied, and not tuned-in most of the time. Speaking of time—we don't have that natural closeness we used to have. You know, just being together, doing things as a couple. I am distressed because I have less and less of your undivided attention.

Most of all, our sex life is different. You don't seem as interested in me sexually and there's something going on in your mind that doesn't include me. We used to make love, now it's just sex. You are into the physical act, but your emotions and mind seem somewhere else. And the way you treat me is drastically different. I can't help but think the old you—the person I committed to spend my life with—would be so embarrassed at the way you relate to me now.

I want a healthy sex life and ours doesn't feel that way to me; in fact it's a turn-off. What's even more insulting is that you get so angry when it doesn't go your way.

I don't know who you are or where your mind is, but it's not on me anymore. It's like we were traveling the same road and then you took a left turn into another world while I kept going straight.

In my mind you took a left turn when you turned to the Internet for stimulation. At first it didn't seem to affect our relationship; you think it even helped. But now you spend more and more time at it. You hide it from me, and you've even lied to me about it. I'm also bothered by the fact that you won't talk about this and you get *defensive when I try to talk about it. I don't know where to go or what to do. You are moving farther away.*

It's frightening to think where our relationship is going.

The Purpose Behind Porn/Chat Room Use

People use pornography and/or chat rooms for a variety of reasons: fun, fantasy, excitement, entertainment, curiosity, comfort, to spice up their love lives, and to learn new techniques. It's also used to alter a mood or offset stress. Some users find the sexual high from the Internet better than physical contact with their partners. Others report an overwhelming anxiety that is only quieted by the pursuit of the next sexual Internet adventure.

No one typically begins viewing porn or visiting chat rooms with the sole intent to hurt their partners, destroy their current sex lives, or engage in socially unacceptable stimulation. Many times the use begins long before a committed relationship is formed.

Technology is an integral part of our lives from an early age. Babies have Facebook pages and toddlers use iPads. Kids Skype Grandma and Grandpa and E-vite their friends to birthday parties. So it begins.

The average age at which a child first views pornography is ten. Yes, you read that correctly, at ten years old! By middle school, a growing number of tweens are sexting and engaging in sexually stimulating electronic conversations. By the time they reach adulthood, electronic erotica is simply a part of life. Most sex education comes from pornography these days. It's anonymous, accessible, affordable, and generally accepted; it's a private pleasure that's seemingly harmless—until it is not.

The Disconnect from Porn/Chat Room Use

Some individuals and couples use erotica in a manner that enhances their lives. As a recreation or pastime, the novelty of erotic variation adds spice and excitement to the sexual repertoire as well as a source of pleasure and stress relief. But it becomes a disconnect when it steals time, attention, energy, and/or commitment from the relationship.

Sexual Internet use can destroy a relationship when: use becomes a compulsion; the increasing need for novel sexual experiences pushes one partner beyond the comfort zone; electronic stimulation evokes brain changes that destroy attraction for the partner; it creates shame or self-loathing in the user; it leads to acting out with other real partners without the consent and cooperation of the committed partner.

The biggest threat with sexual Internet use is that it sneaks up on you. With over 40 million users in the United States it's easy to see it as an acceptable part of life. In the past, porn was expensive and difficult to obtain. (You had to visit a store and risk being seen by a relative or the rector.) Now, in seconds you can have it in front of you—it's that accessible, as well as affordable and anonymous.

The acceptable, accessible, affordable, and anonymous nature of pornography/chatting is pretty well understood, but the fifth "A," addictive, is not. Addiction is the most lethal aspect of all.

Because sex is directly related to survival (the *sine qua non* of the species) it is fueled by dopamine, which is the "gotta-have-it" neurochemical that activates reward circuits in the brain. Dopamine is a motivator; it is the craving signal that makes you want to eat, drink, achieve goals, have sex, explore, even take risks—all necessary for survival.

Dopamine is never satisfied, always taking pleasure in pursuing goals and seeking something new. Dopamine keeps you focused on a particular target, but once you've achieved it, your interests shift to the next goal. Ironically, the more you get the more you want. You begin to see where online pornography and chatting, with unlimited novelty, can far surpass the range of sexual experiences most couples can create.

Extensive porn use and Internet chatting actually *change* your arousal template (what turns you on). Over time, what would normally be sexually stimulating no longer does the trick. Your brain needs something different, more personal or provocative, perhaps more dangerous or even disgusting to get your attention.

Eventually what feels "normal" is outside the user's original acceptable range and the arousal template is changed drastically. This is also where shame and self-loathing enter the picture.

An arousal template created by porn or chatting does not include your partner. Research shows that over time the user loses attraction for the real-life partner, has more difficulty becoming aroused and reaching orgasm, looks at the partner as an object rather than a person, and if continued, the user eventually will seek similar, real-life sexual experiences.

Well over half of all divorces cite use of Internet porn as a significant cause of the breakup. Internet and porn use continue to play an ever-increasing role in relationship splits.

Transforming Porn/Chat Room Use

If the use of pornography/chatting is tearing your relationship apart, it might be best to begin the transformation by viewing it as a bad brain habit instead of a moral failure. The bad news is, the Internet changes your brain. The good news is, you can change it back.

Depending upon your level of use, transforming your habits might be as simple as going cold turkey and giving your brain time to get over the craving. With mild use, if you stop it completely, the appetite for this type of stimulation will wither away. Users report marked differences in sexual desire after only ninety days of abstinence, especially when accompanied by behavior more in line with their core values.

Couples who want to reset their arousal templates are wise to refocus on alternative, positive aspects of their relationships (joint projects, individual passions, affection, communication) to reinforce their commitments. If your sex life has suffered, abstaining from sex during this same time period also can be helpful.

If you suspect your use of pornography/chatting is more serious, consider the following questions:

- Are you using more now than in the beginning?
- Do you anticipate and/or dwell on the use beforehand?
- When you are not using, are you thinking about using?
- Have you experienced an irresistible urge to use against your conscious wishes?
- Have you made promises or plans to cut back or quit but eventually went back to old patterns?

- Do you have the sense that you are not in complete control of the use?

- Are you spending increasing time in an altered state?

- Have you lied to yourself or others about your use?

- Do you hide your use from your partner (or others)?

- Are you embarrassed about the nature of your use?

- Has the use changed your sexual desires or desire for your partner?

- Are you in denial about the money you are spending on your use?

- Have you missed commitments or declined important invitations because of your use?

If you answered yes to three or more questions, then a more serious look at the role pornography is playing in your life may be warranted. Patrick Carnes, PhD, writes compassionately about pornography addiction in his book, *In the Shadows of the Net*. In the book, as well as his workbook, *Facing the Shadow*, he outlines the steps toward healthy sexuality and change.

Anyone struggling with Internet/porn use can benefit from support groups that focus on recovery. These groups are free and can be visited in person or, yes, on the Internet.

More serious issues may need the help of an addictions professional. It is reassuring to know there are well-trained therapists who can guide you through this difficult transformation.

4

Your Spending Is Tearing Us Apart

I paid some bills and reconciled the bank statement today. I don't understand how you can keep spending when you know how much stress it causes.

No matter how many times we've talked about it, argued about it, even seemingly agreed about it, you keep spending. Yes, I know, there is always a good excuse—but that's just it: It's an excuse to do what you want despite how it affects us.

I'm tired of getting angry and always being the enforcer of this issue. It's exhausting worrying about how much money is going to be gone; how high the credit card bill is going to be; how little we have saved; and what happens in the future. And the guilt! I end up being the one who looks bad in this situation and I'm just trying to help us. You act as if I'm trying to deprive you or ruin your life. You fight me every step of the way and I'm worn out.

Honestly, I don't know where to turn. You spend money you don't have, I don't have, and we don't have together. With no thought, you just do as you please. How can you be so continually irresponsible? Don't you ever even think about the effect on the security of our financial future?

To me, it is so disrespectful. I fear where this situation is taking us. I'm hurt, scared, and angry. I can't trust you anymore; you've betrayed my confidence in your ability to change.

The Purpose Behind Spending

In its simplest form, spending and acquisition are related to survival. We need food, water, and shelter just to get by—not just today, but every day.

To stay motivated, your brain reinforces the act of finding and obtaining with a sense of pleasure. If you come home hungry and find your favorite food in the fridge, you feel a sense of delight. When you are cold and throw on a warm shirt or slide into warm slippers, you feel a sense of comfort. Food, fuel, fun, shoes, shirts, shelter—all of these make up a part of daily subsistence and require some type of spending or procurement. But when spending moves from need to never-ending compulsion, you have crossed the line from helpful to harmful.

People spend for a variety of reasons. For some it's a matter of pure survival. For others it's more about fun or personal fulfillment; you do it because it feels good and lifts your mood. Spending also can promise future happiness, for instance, "This new jacket will make me sexier, more attractive, more professional, more successful. . . ."

For a few people, spending wards off dark feelings of deprivation, depression, or worthlessness. Spending also can be a passive-aggressive way of getting back at someone or something. Sometimes spending is a reward for working hard, or simply feeling like you deserve it whether you can afford it or not.

The most common reason people overspend is habit. You see it. You want it. You get it. Despite times of struggle, by some means you're able to maintain the habit. Conscious choice and delayed gratification are foreign concepts for habitual spenders—it's all about impulse and instant satisfaction.

Oddly, the stress that comes with overspending can be a significant part of a downward-spiraling pattern. As stress builds up so does the need for relief. Spending is a quick fix and temporary respite. When you use spending as a coping strategy to suppress unwanted feelings, you have entered the danger zone. This stress-and-spend cycle has all the indicators of an addiction and can cause serious harm.

The Disconnect from Spending

Financial stress is the number one sociological cause of divorce and separation according to many studies. While any extreme around money can cause relational strain, overspending is the most common financial cause of growing apart and an eventual breakup.

It's common for partners to differ at least somewhat in their inclinations toward spending or saving. When spending styles differ within a realistic range, together partners can create a healthy balance between wanting and wasting. But if saving or spending is taken to the extreme, such as when saving becomes deprivation or spending leads to excessive indulgence, then balance gives way to bullying.

Why is money such a powerful issue? Because it's related to your survival. Money provides the means for acquiring essentials such as food, clothing, and shelter. For this reason financial stress is greater stress; financial stress literally feels life threatening.

Anyone who has been broke, homeless, hungry, or embarrassed by financial circumstances will tell you that financial stress is a unique type of pain. When your partner repeatedly inflicts this pain upon you, and when unilateral financial decisions make your life miserable, you will find it increasingly difficult to trust the person responsible for this anguish.

Love is one thing in a relationship but safety and solace are another. When you cannot rely on your partner to protect you from harm—physical, emotional, or financial—you no longer can feel close or connected.

Transforming Overspending

Depending upon the severity of financial stress and the strength of your commitment and communication skills, transforming spending habits can be as simple as making a budget or as strident as seeking treatment for compulsion and addiction. Regardless, the principles of change are the same:

- ♥ You must work as a team without shame or blame.
- ♥ You must each take ownership of your roles (differentiation) in creating the problem.
- ♥ You must implement positive, measurable, specific, and inherently rewarding goals.

We are going to ask you to put a heart around yourself and your partner through each step toward transformation (more about this in Chapter 21). This means to surround the problem with love and kindness, even though you might be coming from two different positions. Compassion and appreciation can make any change easier.

One general fact might help motivate you both toward a different way of spending: The most common way to become a millionaire is for two people to get together, stay together, and live beneath their means. Most wealth comes the old-fashioned way—hard work and healthy habits. Follow these steps to get started:

Step One: Determine why you spend. What situations, feelings, thoughts, and impulses precede any purchase? This is vital. Understanding motivation will direct you toward successful strategies for redirecting or correcting.

Step Two: Make an assessment. Take a realistic look at income and spending. Do this together; agree to the no-shame-or-blame strategy; put it in writing. You must determine how much money comes in and goes out. Take time to appreciate your partner's participation and perspective.

Step Three: Track your spending. This sucks for most people. It's depressing (that's why we use denial!), frightening, humbling, and infuriating. It takes discipline, time, and tempts you to lie—but there is no substitute for accountability. Any plan without tracking likely will fail. Setbacks are normal. Acknowledge and appreciate each other's commitment to change.

Step Four: Separate needs and wants—and tailor your spending accordingly. Do I *need* it or just *want* it? Is this purchase in line with our spending plan? Will I die if I don't have it? Am I buying this for the feeling it gives me? Reinforce each other's progress with appreciation.

Step Five: (Could be Step One.) Don't hesitate to get professional guidance. Whether it's an app or appointment, having an objective, unbiased opinion can take pressure off your relationship and expedite your goals. You are not the first to be in this situation and many, many before you have created any number of effective strategies. There are fine financial counselors to help you move toward healthy spending.

Step Six: Build in reward. Create a game plan with an incentive. Some people are motivated by competition: "I stayed within my allowance better than you thought I could." Others are motivated by saving: "Look how much is in the account now!" Achieving even the smallest goal is rewarding: "It feels good to pay off that credit card." Even challenge can come into play: "Let's see how many days we can go without spending any money."

As mentioned earlier, overspending can become part of a compulsive and even addictive cycle. Here are some questions to ask yourself to see if you've crossed the line.

- ♥ Do you get high or excited just thinking about spending/ shopping?
- ♥ Do you spend money to lift your mood?
- ♥ Have you made a plan to cut back spending but failed to follow through?
- ♥ Have you lied about the amount you spend?
- ♥ Have you spent money that was designated for vital purposes (such as bills, food, expenses, savings)?
- ♥ Do you feel depressed or deprived when you go without spending?
- ♥ Has your spending caused problems in a significant relationship?
- ♥ Have you continued to spend despite serious consequences?

If you answered "yes" to any of these questions, it might be time to seek professional help. The more "yes" answers, the more serious the need for assistance.

Financial health is part of emotional/relational health. Working together to achieve this goal can bring you closer to one another and ensure the future you share will be brighter and better!

5

Your Technology Use Is Tearing Us Apart

When was the last time you gave me an hour of uninterrupted time? Think about it—I mean a block of time where I got your undivided attention? Seems like you are far more interested in your world than our world. It's like you have another life going on and I'm not a part of it.

Lately I've become very familiar with the top of your head because that's what I see most of the time when we're together. Your face, focus, and feelings all go into a gadget. In our relationship technology gets touched more than I do!

A lot of times I don't start a meaningful conversation or even suggest an activity to do together because I know your heart won't be in it or we'll be interrupted. Time with me isn't important to you anymore. Your behavior speaks louder than your words.

Your inattention is truly hurtful. I feel unimportant, neglected, and yes, angry. I'm tired of competing because I know I can't win. You have to make me important again, our relationship important again, and show it with your undivided attention.

I understand relaxing; I understand staying in touch; I understand work; but when our relationship is suffering because you are not paying attention then it has gone too far. Basically your body might be with me but your heart and soul are somewhere else. I'm in our space; you are in cyberspace. I feel like I've been substituted for an electronic device. I could be a robot.

The Purpose Behind Technology Use

One can easily make a case for technology being a necessary part of today's world given the fact that fewer and fewer jobs are technology-free. From homemaking to healthcare, finance to fire-fighting—technology use is a part of work. We use it to stay current and keep abreast of our chosen roles in life. When used wisely technology can speed access, support staying in touch, help you relax, heighten awareness, entertain, and even educate. Couples who get creative find technology can keep those home fires burning even when separated by miles and many other obligations.

It's not really technology use that tears couples apart; it's the misuse—and the line between the two is ambiguous and often a matter of perception. What is convenient for one partner may be a conflict for the other.

Technology use for work, at work, rarely causes problems in relationships. It's when technology use bleeds into time at home that it becomes a problem.

People bring work home via technology for a variety of reasons: because it is a requirement of the job; to avoid being behind the next day; because other co-workers are working after hours; to deal with clients in different time zones; to lighten the load during regular work hours; because work is more interesting than other activities going on; it feels good to use your knowledge and expertise; it helps other co-workers; it keeps you connected to work in a more meaningful way, and so on.

Not all technology use is related to work. We use technology at home for keeping in touch with friends, recreation, learning, socializing, and having fun; our technology use can be a hobby, a habit, a way to manage stress or change our mood. The novelty and entertainment value of technology is virtually unlimited and highly efficient. At your fingertips is a source of stimulation that is accessible, acceptable, affordable, and anonymous if you want it to be. The biggest reasons why people use technology at home is it feels good and it's fun.

The Disconnect from Technology Use

Technology use tears couples apart when time and energy that belongs to the relationship is devoted to a device. Relationships are sustained by undivided attention. When intimate moments are interrupted repeatedly by the ding of a phone or the call of the computer, or when technology gets priority over sustained time alone with one another, then dissolution may not be far behind.

Imagine sitting in a restaurant and spotting a couple across from you looking madly in love. As you picture this couple, what are they doing? You likely see them smiling, leaning in, touching hands, and looking at one another. Most likely you envision them talking and listening to each other with rapt attention.

Now imagine another couple. This time one partner is trying to carry on a conversation but the other is texting. Or one partner is self-disclosing while the other is taking a selfie. How would you describe their connection? What does their behavior say about the relationship?

The difference between these two couples is their level of attunement as well as personal interest. This isn't to imply that all couples need to spend every moment sitting knee-to-knee, gazing into one another's eyes, but moments of connection have to occur on a dependable basis for a relationship to survive and thrive.

When technology use robs the relationship of life-giving energy, when one partner is repeatedly excluded from the other's heart and mind, the couple is at risk for growing apart.

Transforming Technology Use

There is simply no substitute for enjoyable, uninterrupted time together. Transformation won't occur unless you make this happen.

Some couples find it helpful making a schedule, blocking off dedicated times for the relationship with no interference. Others find success by establishing an intimacy zone, such as no technology in the bedroom or during meals.

The most successful plan must involve making your brain a better offer. Most of us use technology because we get a payoff or benefit, and therefore, time together must do the same.

To make any permanent change it's always easier to add positives than eliminate negatives. It's not enough to block off time with no interruption if that time together isn't rewarding. Together, you must plan activities you both enjoy—things that always leave you feeling closer and have enough variety to keep your energy and attention up over time. Here are some quick tips:

- ♥ **Turn off and tune in.** Have quiet times or quiet zones which afford uninterrupted opportunities for connection. No time is sacred until technology is out of sight and earshot.

- ♥ **Make time together enjoyable.** Create a list of activities that are mutually enjoyable and guaranteed to bring you closer together. For example: cooking together; watching a movie; talking about plans and dreams for the future; appreciating one another; learning a new skill; completing projects; exercising; entertaining; remembering fun times; going on a date; sports; snuggling; sex; and dancing.

- ❤ **Move beyond the setbacks.** Forming new habits rarely takes place in a straight line from A to Z. Expect a few awkward times when boredom sets in or temptation calls, even when you slip back into old behaviors. Know this is normal and get back on track with an activity that brings you closer again.

Acknowledge and verbally appreciate any efforts made to focus time and attention on your relationship. Put a heart around yourself and your partner. Catch your partner in the act of doing something right and reward it!

6

Your Work Is Tearing Us Apart

I can't believe you are working late again tonight! You are ALWAYS working, and the only thing that seems to make you happy these days is work, work, work! I can't remember the last time we had a free weekend or just one evening together without you working. Why is your job so important? I know work is necessary to earn a living, but your work consumes your entire life——our entire life. I feel like your work is more important than me and our relationship.

I sound like a broken record, always complaining about how much you work. Sometimes I feel hopeless and wonder if you even want to spend time with me. I want to spend time with you; I need to spend time with you. I wish you would show just half as much interest in me and our relationship as you do your job.

Is this really the relationship you want? I feel like you are married to your work! I don't want this to end in an ultimatum, but I can't take this much longer. I feel abandoned and alone. I need you to make me and our relationship a priority.

Either you don't know how serious this is, what a threat it is to our relationship, or you simply don't care. Either way, your obsession with work is tearing us apart.

The Purpose Behind Work

For most of us, work is necessary for survival, and with millions of people unemployed or underemployed, simply having a job is a major accomplishment. Anyone paying attention knows the term "job security" has become a contradiction in terms because those who don't play by the company rules can be replaced.

In today's economy, the pressure workers feel to produce, stay longer, and be on call 24/7 is very real. With endless deliverables, deadlines, and demands in a highly competitive global economy, practically every job requires more time and energy than forty hours a week at least some of the time. Long hours are mandatory all the time in certain professions. Working too much is the cultural norm in many parts of the world.

Beyond necessity, individuals do work for various reasons. The sense of achievement and purpose that comes from a job well done boosts your confidence and self-worth. In addition, work gives life meaning and the opportunity to make a difference.

There is also a "worker's high" that comes from completing the tasks at hand. Nature rewards you for completion by bathing your brain with endorphins, dopamine, and other feel-good neurochemicals. It's no surprise research shows that people who work later in life are healthier than those who give up their jobs at retirement age.

Work is also a concrete expression of love and commitment. Countless individuals toil away at work they don't enjoy or careers they wouldn't choose again because the job represents an investment in the relationship. One of the deepest pains you can inflict on your partner is to devalue the commitment and contribution of work.

The Disconnect from Work

Starting early in life we are taught to believe the harder you work, the more you succeed. Hard work reaps both personal and financial reward—but not without repercussions. For most of us, working harder means working *longer*, leaving less time and energy for other important areas of life such as friends, hobbies, fun, and of course, relationships.

Most of us struggle to maintain a healthy balance between work and life. However, to successfully maintain a loving relationship, you must *show up and spend positive time together with your partner*. There is no substitute for intimate connection. When you take time and energy that belongs to the relationship and put it into work, your relationship surely will suffer. Though you may be working *for* the relationship, you're taking energy *from* the relationship.

Another reason people work too much is that staying on the job can provide a convenient excuse for escaping a difficult relationship. Why hurry home only to face criticism, shame and blame, anger or negativity? Why not stay at work where you feel valued and appreciated? Work may provide temporary safe shelter, but ultimately work won't protect you from the relationship storm at home.

Work itself can be an endless storm. Stress created by work can sabotage even the strongest relationships. Stress floods your body with cortisol and over time burns through feel-good neurochemicals faster than your body can replace them. Stay stressed long enough and most likely you will be depressed. Biochemical imbalance makes it almost impossible to have fun or maintain a happy, healthy emotional state. Stress from work can make you tired, cranky, and not much fun to be around—on the job or on the couch.

Far too many couples are stuck in the weariness of work with little hope for relief. Somehow we believe relationships can stay alive unattended on the back burner. If you starve the relationship to feed work, the relationship can wither away while longing for the interest, energy, and attention it needs to survive.

Transforming Work

There's a saying: "If you like the results you get, keep doing the same thing; if you don't like the results, do something different!" Doing something different often starts simply by putting a heart around the problem and adjusting your attitude and expectations. Wrapping a problem in compassion shifts your perception from negative to positive, and when you take away shame, criticism, and blame, you can begin addressing the actual problem and move toward positive change.

For example, if you are the one complaining about your partner's work, consider shifting your perception from negative to positive. Show appreciation for the time you do spend together:

"I love seeing you walk in the door."

"When we sit and talk like this I feel loved."

"Having fun together makes me want to make love."

Prioritize and compromise. Certain times in life call for focusing extra energy and hours on work, such as when you're building a new career or establishing credibility in a new job. The challenge is to prioritize work without sacrificing your relationship. Times like these call for compromises in other areas of your life.

For example, your house may not be crystal clean all the time. You may have to hire-out handy work instead of doing household repairs yourself. You might go out to eat more often or bring more take-out meals home. You may have to wait for a few years before starting a new hobby, doing volunteer work, or hosting extended family for the holidays.

What's most important is to make any decision of this nature together, not unilaterally. When you are both invested in your future, even difficult times can pay off in the long run. If you are going to delay gratification, delay it on home or car maintenance instead of your mate.

Move in your partner's direction. Work-related issues cause considerable disagreement for couples. Getting back to agreement takes one step at a time. Here are some suggestions to help you get started:

- ♥ When making a change, convert a negative attitude into a positive one and emphasize your optimistic expectations.
- ♥ Imagine your life with work in balance. What does that look like?
- ♥ What would make you want to work less?
- ♥ How can you and your partner make that happen? Make a list and be specific.
- ♥ Start small and set realistic goals. Making a small plan you'll keep is better than making a big plan you won't. For example:
  - *Set aside Friday evenings for just the two of you to spend together.*
  - *Once a week meet for lunch, just the two of you.*
  - *Once a week sit and have coffee together in the morning before work.*
  - *Once a month take dance lessons together.*

Together you and your partner decide how you want your life to look with work in balance, and then take steps to move toward this new lifestyle. The following exercise can help you identify specific, manageable steps for moving to common ground.

Think of a request or desire you have about work that your partner does not share. Take turns as **Requestor** and **Responder**, spending equal time in each role to improve communication and move in the direction of understanding. Be honest and creative.

Moving in Your Direction

Requestor (Partner #1)	Responder (Partner #2)
1) **Make a request, stating it as clearly and specifically as possible.** *Example: "I would like for you to work less so that we can spend time together."*	2) **Respond by moving in the direction of request: "Would it be moving in your direction if I . . .?"** *Example: "Would it be moving in your direction if I would be home no later than 7:00 PM one day a week for us to spend the evening together?"* If you fully agree to your partner's request, state that now. If you cannot agree to the request as stated, then make a suggestion that is as close to your partner's request as is agreeable with you.
3) **Respond to Partner #2.** *Example: "That's acceptable to me. I also want your commitment that you will be home no later than 7:00 PM once a week without me reminding you."*	4) **Respond to Partner #1.** *Example: "In fact, I'd like your promise that you won't remind me. That you'll trust me to do it. Thursdays are best for me. If you will look at your calendar then we can confirm the day."*
5) **Respond to Partner #2.** *Example: "Thanks, I'll look right now."*	6) **Switch roles.**

It's important to structure your time in an enjoyable way when you begin changing your schedule. When work has been the focus of your time, it's easy to feel bored or useless when you're not working—almost as if you've forgotten how to have a normal life with fun and balance!

Another method for creating a relationship-friendly lifestyle is to ask these questions:

- If my work reflected my core values, how would my weekly schedule look?
- If I made my relationship a priority, how would our weekly schedule look?

One person can make a difference by realigning work with core values, but it's even more beneficial for the relationship when both partners take responsibility for making positive changes. If you want something different, you must do something different.

Reframe and reboot. Life is full of possibilities. One last suggestion for transforming work requires a reframing of ideas and perhaps even a reboot. Don't try this approach without first putting a heart around it!

What if the two of you throw caution to the wind and make a huge change in your work life? Quit your job; start your own business; liquidate your assets and travel for a year; live with friends/family and go back to school; downsize and do nothing for a while; change roles; ask for a drastic change in your present job; or put a time limit on your current work while saving money to make a big change down the road.

Just brainstorming about your options sometimes can put your current choices into perspective. You may not need to change your life as much as you need to change your perception.

If your partner is a true workaholic, you need to ask yourself, how serious is this situation? Is it serious enough that you can't move forward without professional help? You need to have hope about your future, and that may involve creating a hard boundary.

Whatever you decide to do about your work/relationship balance, the key is moving forward with an attitude of love, compassion, and positive energy.

7

Your Sexual Withholding Is Tearing Us Apart

You wonder why I'm distant, angry, and hurt. You wonder why I'm not affectionate—just think about it. How would you feel if you reached out to me for sex and I turned my back, pushed you away, or made lame excuses to avoid any romantic or sexual time together? How about if I went day after day ignoring your sexual needs?

It's hard for me to feel like helping you or supporting you when you're so insensitive. Problem is, it takes two of us to be sexual but only one person (you!) to say no. You have the power to stop our sex life and you have used that power at the risk of our happiness.

You must not feel what I feel when we go without sex. I can't help but believe if you knew how physically, emotionally, and psychologically uncomfortable it is for me that you would feel more guilty about your resistance. Or maybe you just don't care; maybe you don't care about sex and don't care about me. Whatever the reason, I'm not happy about it and you should understand why I'm upset.

The Purpose of Sexual Withholding

People withhold sex for a variety of reasons. Sometimes it's simply a difference in sexual desire: one partner wants sex twice a week and the other prefers twice a month. (Those are the two most common frequency preferences among couples, by the way.)

Some partners don't enjoy the same sexual activities and therefore resist any sexual contact at all. They lack effective communication skills as well as suggestions for sexual techniques that could lead to mutual enjoyment.

A significant number of couples simply don't make time for sex. They lead busy lives with little relaxation or quiet moments together.

Some partners simply aren't interested in sex and feel justified in ignoring their partner's needs—although this is far rarer than you might believe. Given the right situation almost everyone enjoys sex.

If the partner who initiates sex more often exhibits offensive behavior, such as acting in an angry or defensive manner, this may serve as a turn-off and justification for the other partner to withhold sexual contact. Without effective communication skills a cold war may ensue.

Easily, the most common reason partners withhold sex is lack of information related to healthy, fun, sexual practices. They don't know what turns them on and therefore cannot provide their partners with constructive information that would lead to mutual satisfaction. They may never have come close to experiencing their own sexual potential.

The Disconnect from Sexual Withholding

Early in a relationship, with novelty fueling the libido, sexual desire and receptivity run high for most couples. Over the course of time normal differences evolve, requiring skills and knowledge to navigate. Unfortunately, not all individuals or couples are equipped to manage these sexual changes.

When reality falls short of expectations, disappointment sets in. In the beginning of a relationship it appears as if you both have the same desires, similar interests in sex, and are tuned in to one another's needs in an almost perfect manner. Managing your intimate love life takes little or no effort at all. This romantic love stage fosters the belief that it will always be this way. When normal differences emerge, disenchantment follows. How you manage this common post-rapture stage of love will determine how connected or disconnected you are as a couple.

Disconnection occurs when curiosity, caring, compassion, and open communication are replaced with criticism, control, blame, bullying, defensiveness, defiance, withdrawal, withholding, anger, or avoidance.

Transforming Sexual Withholding

Most people live a lifetime and never experience the full pleasure of their sexual potential—or the potential of the partnership. Unaware of sexual styles as well as the differing pathways to arousal, they stay stuck in old patterns and parochial views. Transformation requires a new perspective beginning with commitment to creating a passionate relationship together.

Sexual withholding can be a little problem or a big problem, and transformation must be congruent with the level of severity.

If you are just out of practice and need to get back on track, reignite your sex life with these words of wisdom:

- ♥ Set mutually established sensual/sexual goals for your relationship.
- ♥ Start with small, doable goals.
- ♥ Make time for sex. Block off private, uninterrupted periods and make these commitments sacred.

- ♥ Become an expert in your own sexual arousal and desire.
- ♥ Establish a safe way of talking about sex.
- ♥ Accept and honor differences between the two of you.
- ♥ Understand that half the population doesn't feel like having sex until they are already having sex.
- ♥ Just say yes!

Most couples agree that sex is important to the care and feeding of a relationship, but they get stuck around the "will we or won't we have sex" stage. Take away the tension and just say yes! Replace withholding with a commitment to be available as a sexual/sensual/intimate partner whenever either of you has the desire.

You say when, I say how. There are many, many ways to be sexual. From the quickie to the weekend sex fest, couples run the gamut when it comes to sensual pleasure. Get in the habit of expanding your sexual repertoire in terms of time, attention, and technique.

If the issues between the two of you are more complicated than just getting off track, then you might need to address the unresolved issues that are contaminating your sex life:

- ♥ Set aside time to talk and listen in a calm, respectful manner.
- ♥ Practice replacing criticism with asking specifically for what you want.
- ♥ Anytime your partner comes close to pleasing you, acknowledge the act with a smile, touch, or "Thank you!"
- ♥ Consult a third party—read one of our books! Use *Hot Monogamy* or *You Can Make It Happen* as a study guide for your relationship.

If sex has become a deal-breaker, or if the two of you are growing further apart, *consult a specialist ASAP*. There is no substitute for professional support when it comes to sexual issues that threaten your relationship. Counseling doesn't have to go on forever or cost a fortune. Be sure to work with a therapist who has been trained in relationship counseling as well as sexuality. There's not a better way to invest in your home improvement!

8

Your Lack of Financial Contribution Is Tearing Us Apart

I would feel far more relaxed, loved, and supported if you made a greater financial contribution to our relationship. Maybe you don't feel the stress I do; maybe you're doing your best—but it doesn't look that way to me. You have so much talent and potential that could bring in more money. I want you to use it to improve our life as well as our relationship.

It is becoming increasingly difficult to understand why you don't see how a greater contribution from you would improve our life together. I personally believe you'd also feel better about yourself.

I can't continue to carry so much of the burden without feeling unloved and unsupported. It's tough to be sensitive to your needs when it doesn't look like you are sensitive to my needs—our needs. The relationship doesn't feel fair to me.

If you made more of a financial contribution, I would feel better about you as an invested partner in our relationship. It can't be enjoyable for you to know how unhappy I am, and this isn't easy for me to say, let alone think or feel.

I want to feel good about you again. I want to feel hopeful about us again and to get back to the fun and freedom we felt in the beginning of our relationship. Please find a way to bring in more money.

The Purpose Behind Lack of
Financial Contribution

Some people are not motivated primarily by money. Money is a means to an end, not the end itself. The reward in their chosen work may be reflected in how much they enjoy it, not how much they earn. The satisfaction they feel and subsequently bring to the relationship seems just as important as an increase in salary.

Another reason people stay in lower-paying jobs is they feel confident in their abilities for those particular jobs and are reticent to change. If the job offers a relaxed or comfortable work environment, this fact may carry a lot of weight. Lack of stress, enjoying the people you work with, feeling like you're part of a team, or making an important difference all contribute to job satisfaction and add value to your life, but not necessarily more money to your bank account.

In a different scenario, a partner may choose to stay in a situation that lacks more financial contribution to avoid fear of failure or change. If you've been out of the job market for a while, getting back in can feel like jumping on a moving train. In addition, if the job market is weak, it may feel imprudent to move toward different employment and smart to hold on to any job you have. When unemployment is high, so many workers are waiting for your job. Giving up your position or even letting the word get out that you're looking for another job may be more of a risk than you're willing to take.

Another reason why making more of a financial contribution can be difficult, depending upon your chosen field, is that there may be an inherent economic limit to the pay grade. Your spouse may believe you deserve more money, but the reality of your salary increasing past a certain limit is slim and none. It's difficult to give up an entire career because of money, especially when you've paid a lot of time and money to educate or train for it.

So far we've mentioned rather practical reasons behind lack of financial contribution, but we would be remiss if we didn't include the inertia that comes from depression, physical illness, or anxiety beyond ordinary fear of failure. The real issue may be the underlying personal stress unseen by others, even the partner.

Finally, it's important to remember not everyone's highest and best use of talent is being an economic engine. Some partners might not add more money to the joint bank account because they believe they add value to the relationship in other ways. Homemaking, child care, maintenance, shopping, entertaining, managing the social calendar, keeping up with family, repairs, and so on—all have an economic value. These necessary tasks make a major contribution to quality of life and to many they are priceless. Taking a job that would eliminate or greatly reduce these contributions may seem neither wise nor fiscally smart.

The Disconnect from Lack of Financial Contribution

One of the primary reasons people commit to a relationship is to gain a partner to share the pleasures and shoulder the struggles. When the contribution is out of balance, it's as if part of the relationship dies, or goes missing. The partner carrying a disproportionate share of the responsibility can feel abandoned, disrespected, or resentful.

Resentment is a dangerous emotion in relationships. It is a form of anger based on the belief that you have been wronged and don't have a complete choice in the situation. It speaks of an uninvited inequality—often born in occasions when a unilateral decision's been made by one partner but affects both—such as saying no to sex, refusing to visit the in-laws, or yelling at the kids.

When resentment is connected to money it carries extra weight because money isn't just a currency. Money represents security, wealth, and options; it can symbolize success, accomplishment, and mastery. In relationships money carries all the significance listed above but in addition can represent love, support, thoughtfulness, commitment, comfort, entitlement, power, authority, happiness, independence, freedom, and opportunity. The downside is that it also can be connected to shame, humiliation, inadequacy, fear, failure, and vulnerability. This is why deeper issues emerge when the subject is money.

When you can't trust your partner with your deepest feelings, when you feel unsupported in a vital part of life, or when you are alone with the responsibility of financial support, then relationship trust is violated and connection is weakened.

Transforming Your Lack of Financial Contribution

The first step toward change begins with an agreement to work as a team. Instead of "your problem" or "my problem," view it as a joint project and imagine celebrating a very positive outcome together. Support each other as you work through these steps:

- ♥ Acknowledge that this is a common issue faced by many couples and be assured that working together toward a satisfying solution will make your commitment stronger and love more enduring.

- ♥ Make a list of non-financial contributions you make to the relationship. For example: cooking, maintenance, initiating fun, planning entertainment, taking care of kids, making home look beautiful, being an excited sex partner, taking care of family, remembering birthdays—every single item is significant!

- ♥ Cross the bridge into your partner's world, and without help, make a list of what your partner contributes to the relationship.

- ♥ Thank your partner aloud for each item. If you want extra points, tell your partner what it means to *you*.

- ♥ Identify the core issue. Is the concern related to money or commitment to the relationship? Is the concern, "You're having fun but I'm not?" Determining the bottom line will help you formulate a successful plan and solution.

- ♥ Decide on realistic goals and a timetable.

- ♥ Block off a period of uninterrupted time to look at the facts concerning your finances. Ninety minutes might be a reasonable starting point. You will not finish in this time but it will not exhaust you if managed with calm communication and compassion.

- ♥ Get out the calculator. Look at your income and expenses. Get the facts.

- ♥ If overspending is the issue, look at Chapter 4 in this book and follow the steps to change.

- ❥ Brainstorm possible solutions. With brainstorming, no option is discounted. Let the sky be the limit.

- ❥ If a job change is considered, get a realistic look at the cost versus benefits. Check for hidden costs, e.g. commuting, (estimated $800 per mile per year by car), parking, child-care, meal costs, wardrobe, paying for tasks you do your-self like walking the dog and cleaning your house, loss of income between jobs.

- ❥ With a different job, remember that salary is just one part of the equation. Consider health benefits, incentive pay, flexibility, retirement plans, vacation, taxes, etc.

- ❥ Acknowledge that earning money is a complex task; for some it comes easy, for others it's very difficult. The first step toward change may be to identify any underlying rea-sons why contributing more money creates resistance.

If the thought of addressing this issue raises too much anxiety or you fear the repercussions on your relationship, seek help. Relationship counselors are well-trained to help you navigate difficult subjects such as finances.

9

Your Overinvolved Parenting Is Tearing Us Apart

I hate to even bring it up because I know it's a sore subject, but I wish you had as much time and energy for being my partner as you do for being a parent (or grandparent). There always seems to be enough money or interest or excitement, except when it comes to our relationship. I appreciate your dedication, but I want a partner; I don't think they are mutually exclusive.

The most troubling part of this issue is I feel like I am not your best friend or your confidant; it doesn't even feel like I'm your social partner; and romance or affection are out of the question when you are in your parent mind-set—and that's most of the time. Am I jealous? Yes. Because you have put a child in the role you promised to me. Think about how many kid activities you plan and take part in and how many are just for the two of us to have fun. That says it all!

The Purpose Behind Overinvolved Parenting

Parents who are overinvolved with kids, such as doing activities that the kids can do for themselves, do it for a variety of reasons. Sometimes as parents we overfunction out of habit, "That's the way I was raised," or to overcompensate, "My mom/dad never helped me. . . ." Other times, we do it out of fear, "I don't want him/her to be mad at me," or we project our own anxiety on the child, "I don't want him/her to fail so I'll help." Some of us are overinvolved because parenting is the one job we believe we do well.

We also can be overinvolved parents just because we love to give and feel needed. We give our own pleasure precedence over fostering independence and competence in our children.

If you ask about the purpose behind any particular parenting style you'll likely get an answer like, "I'm doing my best to raise happy, healthy children who will grow up to be responsible adults." Interestingly there are many different ways to accomplish this goal, and rarely do two people completely agree on how to go about it. Parenting has its rewards as well as responsibilities, and as individuals, we perform our roles as mom or dad in different ways. Regardless of the style, raising children requires some involvement and participation. The issue is where to draw the line.

The Disconnect from Overinvolved Parenting

Partnering is a primary part of parenting. Children fare best in families where the parents have strong, loving, and supportive relationships.

When the partnership is neglected, with time and energy consistently going toward parenting at the expense of the love relationship, this sends a strong message not only to the neglected partner but also to the children. A parent who indulges the children while ignoring the partnership basically is saying, "You are not important, and the children count more than our relationship." It's easy for the left-out partner to feel like a failure, rejected, or abandoned. Sometimes the partner even feels jealous that a child is getting the time and attention that was promised to the spousal relationship. These resentments build a wedge, which over time grows into disconnection.

Transforming Your Parenting Style

There is very good news in the parenting-partnering dilemma. Being a good parent and a good partner are not mutually exclusive. The first step is to get the roles straight.

Parenting is about providing love, structure, protection, guidance, and instruction; however, before you perform any act for a child (regardless of age) ask yourself these questions:

- ♥ Can my child do it alone?
- ♥ Am I robbing my child of the opportunity to learn an important lesson or task?
- ♥ Am I meeting my child's needs or my needs?

Partnering is about being a lover, best friend, confidant, social partner, and financial partner. When you turn to a child to meet your adult emotional needs, such as being a best friend or confidant, you have put the child in the role of a partner. When your social life focuses around child activities, you have put the child in the role of the partner.

When you spend all of your discretionary time meeting the needs of a child while leaving little or none for your relationship, you have put the child in the role of a partner. Commitment to the relationship means that your partner has the right to expect you to meet some of his/her needs at least some of the time. Your partner has the right to expect you to make the love relationship a priority.

When making a transformation be sure to remember that *modeling a healthy, happy partnership is a major part of parenting*. It's one of the greatest gifts you can give your children! As counterintuitive as it might seem to the overinvolved partner, focusing on your love relationship will make you a better parent.

10

Your Controlling Behavior Is Tearing Us Apart

I feel like I'm living in a vice. I can't move right or left, forward or backward, without you getting upset or somehow correcting me. I've avoided this subject for a long time because I don't want your anger, your criticism, or your silent treatment, but I'm worn out and worried that it's getting worse.

Living with you is not fun anymore; in fact it's like walking on eggshells. I find myself giving up more and more of my life because of your "my way or the highway" attitude.

You don't trust me or how I do things. Or maybe you just think I'm stupid. You act like your opinion is always the right one and mine doesn't matter. I've given up so many things that are important to me just to keep peace with you—but it's never enough. You keep making up new rules and limiting more of my behavior. The only time you are nice to me is when you are in charge and I'm in chains.

If this sounds like an exaggeration, please think about it. Think about how many of my friends and family you don't like and don't want me spending time with; how many of my activities I've cut short or cut out because you disapprove; how many times I've tried to please you and only gotten your criticism and complaints; and how many times you've gotten angry just because I did something my way instead of your way. And then there's the biggest sin I commit—having fun without you. I really pay for that one.

I know you are smart. I know you have good ideas, and most of the time I know you love me, but your need to control my behavior is suffocating me and snuffing the life out of our relationship.

The Purpose Behind Controlling Behavior

The most common reason why we try to control another person's behavior is to manage our own anxiety or insecurity. We feel safer and less vulnerable when everything happens as expected. This fact easily goes unnoticed because it's largely *unconscious*. What others see as controlling is often seen as doing the right thing to the person in control, or at least doing it in a better way.

Those blamed for being controlling are often confused by this accusation. They see what they believe to be the best course of action and are incredulous when others don't see it the same way. Motivated by the desire to help, partners who are controlling come on strong with suggestions and work hard to gain compliance.

Controlling behavior also can be compensation for a time or situation when the partner had no control such as growing up, a stressful job, or a former relationship. Living without personal control can increase the motivation to seize control wherever possible.

The most severe forms of control are motivated by emotional dysregulation, which is the inability to manage our own feelings. In an attempt to avoid the fear of abandonment or the shame of inadequacy, the controlling partner resorts to extreme emotions such as anger, rage, threats, and even emotional or physical abuse.

The Disconnect from Controlling Behavior

When relationships work, they are better than ever in this day and age. The primary difference in twenty-first century couples and those in the past is the level of equality, equity, freedom, and autonomy. Relationships thrive when each individual has the liberty to develop and grow as a person and a partner. This evolving process generates energy that keeps both partners interested and excited about a future together.

When one partner tries to control or limit the other's choices, excitement is replaced by resentment, which is the number one cause of growing apart, and growing apart is cited as the most common reason for divorce and separation.

Once resentment enters a relationship, excitement fades, passion wanes, and anger is never far behind. Good feelings and effective communication go out the window, while criticism, defensiveness, and withdrawal seep in. When negative exchanges begin to outweigh the positives, the relationship is in serious trouble of tearing apart.

Transforming Controlling Behavior

Sometimes controlling behavior is simply a habit. The best way to break a habit is to form a new one. Developing a "no advice" policy might be just the right approach to replace the old pattern.

As soon as you catch yourself trying to control your partner, stop and apologize: "There, I did it again, I'm sorry." Apology goes a long way to correct the pattern and reconnect to your partner.

Instead of ordering, directing, or trying to influence your partner, simply say one word: "Oh." This noncommittal stance puts you in a place of curiosity, not correction. Saying "Oh" makes you pause and think, perhaps even reflecting on your partner's point of view. You might just discover a great deal of wisdom in your partner's perspective—especially if you're willing to learn as well as love.

Most controlling behavior is fueled by anxiety or fear; therefore, you must learn to manage those feelings within yourself instead of trying to manage your partner's behavior. Emotional regulation gives you control of what happens in your mind and your own behavior. Trying to control your partner's life will wear you out and tear down your relationship.

A surefire strategy to which you both can agree is to *stop doing what doesn't work*. If the old pattern of controlling starts up, just stop. Call a time-out. If even one partner changes the pattern, the old pattern ceases. You can't have an argument over control when one person refuses to participate.

If you're the partner feeling controlled, then it's your responsibility to speak up! Silence enables the behavior to continue. You might be more aware of the controlling behavior than your partner. Work together to agree upon a kind way to signal when the pattern re-emerges. Develop a redirect strategy to replace the old habits. For example: "When I lift my hand in the stop position, I'd like you to be quiet and let me finish what I am doing."

If you do not feel safe or competent to talk with your partner about the issue of control, take this as a sign to seek professional help.

11

Your Sexual Demands Are Tearing Us Apart

Even when you aren't talking I can feel your demands for sex. Yes, I used the right word—demands. It's like sex is your right and you feel entitled to claim that right at any time, regardless of how you treat me and regardless of what I want and need at the time. To you, sexual urgency equals an emergency.

Is sex all I'm good for? Do you even see past the sex? If you do, I'm missing something. When you look at me, I feel like you only see my body and what you can get out of me sexually. You never see **me**. How do you think that makes me feel? Am I just a body here to service you? Am I only good for sex?

I know you say you love me, but I do not feel loved. There's never time for me personally—or for us for that matter. It's all about you and your sexual needs.

You wonder why I'm silent, why I don't talk or smile or laugh anymore. Our relationship is not fun for me. In fact, I think this situation is a lot more serious than you know.

The saddest part of it all is that I want sex as well. But I want sex to be more than a response to your demands. I want to connect with you and to be aroused together. I want sex to be a way we express our love. It can be hot; it can be raucous; but I want it to be about both of us.

Your demand deadens my desire. I miss the passion—I want it back!

The Purpose Behind Sexual Demands

Human sexuality has a huge responsibility playing a primary role in the survival of our species (meet, mate, procreate). Yet the act of sex is far more than a procreation plan; it's a powerful source of pleasure and capable of forging a magnificent bond between two people. For these and so many other reasons—including fun!—it makes sense to want sex.

Most everyone wants sex, but *wanting* sex and *desiring* sex are two different things. Half the population walks around with bodies ready for sex; they have ongoing sexual desire that intensifies over time. The other half of the population wants sex, but sexual desire comes by way of feeling calm and connected with their partners. For these individuals, sexual desire grows to a heightened state only through intimacy. Half of all partners have to feel connected to have sex; the other 50 percent have to have sex to feel connected!

Unmet sexual needs create a significant problem for individuals as well as couples in relationships. When desire builds up and goes without release, sexual sensations become more physically, emotionally, and psychologically uncomfortable—even painful. Increasing desire seeps into your thoughts, even your dreams. It becomes your primary focus, rendering many high-desire partners unable to concentrate on anything else. Pent-up sexual desire makes you angry, irritable, and unhappy.

Unmet sexual needs paired with inattention from your partner equals a very tense relationship. When your pain worsens by the minute and your partner has the remedy, it's hard for the high-desire person to understand the other's level of insensitivity in withholding relief.

The Disconnect from Sexual Demands

When your partner ignores your need, whether for sex or sensitivity, it becomes increasingly difficult to feel close and connected. When you don't listen when I talk, respond when I touch, or care when I hurt—how can I feel loved?

We are all a little different and somewhat unique in our desire for sex. For some, desire for sex comes after intimacy. For others, desire for intimacy comes after sex. Others say, "I want it all." Regardless, when our needs go unmet we experience pain, and this discomfort creates a breach in the relationship.

It takes the participation of two people to experience the ecstasy of mutual sexual pleasure, and it takes two people to experience the magic of emotional intimacy. Because of this, we each need our partner's full cooperation to feel satisfied in a relationship. Therefore, when one person withholds sex or the other withholds intimacy, that person becomes the hindrance to any hope for happiness. You begin to see how resentment builds and ultimately can create disconnection.

Transforming Sexual Demands

Most partners want both emotional and sexual intimacy, but the question is: How will you negotiate a mutually satisfying way to get both? Transformation can easily begin by looking at the facts.

Fact #1—*Transformation doesn't have to take a lot of time.*

What are we really talking about in terms of time and energy when it comes to sexual, verbal, or emotional intimacy? Probably not hours upon hours but more like minutes upon minutes.

A loving touch, ten minutes of listening, a romantic surprise, or an unexpected quickie—all can begin the transformation from demanding to mutual delight.

Fact #2—*You have to play to your audience.*

If sexual demands are tearing your relationship apart it's highly likely that you and your partner have different sexual styles. What turns one of you on may not do it for the other. Doing more chores may not sound like foreplay to you, but if it gives your partner time to relax and get ready for sex, that's what you need to do! Talking about your day may seem like a waste of time, but if it draws your partner closer, that's what you need to do.

Fact #3—*It's okay to ask.*

If you haven't a clue what turns your partner on, don't be afraid to ask. *But,* don't ask unless you are *truly* interested in the answer and are motivated to be a loving, cooperative participant. When you ask, it's always best to get at least three good answers; this way you both avoid the demand trap. With three options, most individuals can easily comply with one or more. It's also fine to ask: "Would this be a turn-on for you . . . ?"

Fact #4—*Working as a team prevents tearing apart.*

If the two of you can create a common goal, such as having a mutually satisfying sexual relationship, then work together toward that goal. The end result will be highly rewarding. A sample plan might include some of the following:

- ♥ I feel most sexual desire for you when I . . .
- ♥ I feel most sexual desire for you when you . . .
- ♥ It puts me in the mood for sex when we . . .
- ♥ I am best at listening when I . . .
- ♥ I am best at listening when you . . .
- ♥ I feel emotionally closest to you when I . . .
- ♥ I feel emotionally closest to you when you . . .
- ♥ I feel emotionally closest to you when we . . .

Fact #5—*Sometimes simple is best.*

This just might solve the issue in short order. Ask your partner, "Tell me how to express my sexual desire without turning it into a demand." Then do it.

Fact #6—*Sex is a normal request in a committed love relationship.*

You might be shocked at how many couples who ultimately break up expect monogamy without sexual mutuality. It's like, "I expect you to be monogamous, but don't expect me to meet your sexual needs." How does that work? Not well!

If neither of you wants sex and you are not having sex, no problem. But most couples want the enormous benefits sex gives the relationship (bonding, protectiveness, calmness, joy, ecstasy, and sensuality). It's vital that the two of you find a way to navigate the sexual seas to enjoy some smooth sailing.

12

Your Distance
Is Tearing Us
Apart

Where are you? It's like you're always gone. Even when you are here you are not really here! Either you're at work, preoccupied in your own head, or focused on some gadget. It's as if I don't exist in your world. I am so tired of being alone in this relationship.

Do you have any idea how it feels to be with someone who is always distant and unavailable? I could just as well be single.

And then on top of that, you walk out the door as soon as I open my mouth. I get the same reaction whether I rage at you or run from you. No matter how patient or provocative I am you just remain in your own world—one that excludes me.

I wish you really understood how lonely I feel. I'm hurting and anxious and, yes, I'm angry. But my fear is that it doesn't matter to you anyway.

The Purpose Behind Distance

Distance is a defense. When you feel hurt, hopeless, embarrassed, enraged, overwhelmed, overpowered, anxious, alarmed, sad, or scared, detachment can calm your nervous system and regulate your emotions. Although your brain is hardwired for connection, it's also hardwired for protection.

As humans, we have the brilliant capacity to scan for danger twenty-four hours a day without even thinking about it. Any real or perceived danger sounds an alarm and your internal protection system takes over automatically. You may seek distance to gain the time and space to think, make a plan, or gather strength to re-engage. Regardless, distancing is a way of retreating into safety and part of your survival strategy. This automatic response to danger—never to give up entirely—is vital.

For many people distancing behavior feels very normal. Introverts, for example, need time alone to recharge and gather strength for engaging in relationships. When distancing is part of your inherent personality and temperament, it's encoded in your DNA. Sometimes the need for solitude isn't a defense, but rather an innate personal style that doesn't change much over time.

Moving toward a new interest can shift your focus, and that can look a lot like distance. A new smartphone shifts your attention away from the old model. Fascination with a new job, hobby, or friendship can divert energy away from your relationship. Shifting your focus may not be intentional, but attention and energy are *finite*—there's only so much available. When you focus attention in a new area, you take away interest and energy from another.

The Disconnect from Distance

Relationships require care, and part of that responsibility includes showing up and spending positive time together. If you don't tend to these needs, your relationship will suffer and leave you both feeling distressed. Some people handle distress by turning their energy out—they fight, complain, criticize, or pursue. Others manage distress by turning their energy in: they become preoccupied, silent, solitary, or separate. Sometimes, individuals freeze, play dead, or give up. Giving up is the ultimate distancing behavior.

Distancing itself doesn't cause disconnection in relationships. Some of us need time alone to re-energize and be present for relationship. Retreat without a strategy for re-engagement can be lethal. However, it takes two partners to tango in a relationship; one engaged partner is like one hand clapping. If one partner repeatedly fails to show up, tune in, understand, and respond caringly, then the relationship is certain to rip apart.

When distancing takes the place of physical presence; when aloofness replaces focused attention; when detachment derails the desire to understand; and when coldness exists where there should be compassion, the relationship is lifeless—dead in the water.

Transforming Distance

If your partner displays distancing behavior, the best advice may be: *do not take it personally*. That's easy for some, more difficult for others. Either way the message is essential because your partner's withdrawal may not be so much *about you*, even though it certainly affects you.

Distancing behavior can be an old habit carried over from childhood, adolescence, or a previous relationship. The human brain looks for patterns. *We tend to see what we've already seen; feel what we've already felt; and do what we've already done.* For example, your former partner may have been controlling, causing you to retreat to maintain your autonomy. Self-preservation may have put you on guard, defending against coercion and being sensitive to any act interpreted (or misinterpreted) as control. Be careful not to interpret your current partner's behavior errone-ously by confusing it with any past experiences.

Many of us learned to distance ourselves early in childhood, unconsciously responding to whether our caregivers were happy, calm, stressed, sad, or angry. When they were happy, we were happy; when they were stressed, we were stressed. Children often cope using distancing behavior. The point here isn't to blame your parents or your history, but to acknowledge when distancing is an inconvenient response to events from your past.

If distancing is an old habit in need of a new solution, here are some suggestions:

Feel the feeling but do the right thing. If you recognize that withdrawing is an empty habit with potential to wreck your relationship, you can change the bad habit by forming a new one. When you feel the urge to move away, make a new plan. When you realize you have moved away, acknowledge the behavior and make a new plan.

A new plan should move you in the right direction. To determine what is right for any situation you can ask yourself:

- ♥ "What is best for the relationship?" Then do it.
- ♥ "What can I do to calm myself and still be in the relationship?" Then do it.

You can't always consciously control the urge to move away, but you can control how you manage that urge. By mindfully choosing your responses, you can honor your need for safety, solitude, and solace without endangering your relationship.

Make sure pursuing behavior isn't creating the distance. Sometimes distancing behavior is a knee-jerk response to a partner who is perpetually pursuant. You have to retreat to breathe, think, or gather your senses. You can't move toward your partner because your partner has already demanded, expected, or filled up the space.

Pursuers often think they are more available for relationships, but in reality they can cause just as much of a disconnect as the distancer. They fear separation yet their behavior can drive a partner away.

The heart of the pursuer is often filled with anxiety and fear of abandonment. Pursuers have difficulty trusting a partner's love, but most of all they don't take in the affection, attention, and care from their partners. They are programmed for longing and defended against receiving love. They focus on what they don't have instead of savoring what they do have, which can create hopelessness and helplessness in the other partner.

If pursuing is present, here are some tips:

- ❤ **Count your blessings.** Yes, name them one by one. Make this a daily habit.

- ❤ **Express appreciation to your partner in words, deeds, and by going on record.** Write down what you like, love, and appreciate. Make it a record for you both to review. When you acknowledge gratitude you're not only encouraging your partner to increase this behavior, you're also reminding yourself that you got something! Just like writing a thank-you note reminds you of the gift, expressing appreciation reminds you both of your love.

- ❤ **Stop and breathe.** When you feel like pursuing, such as asking questions, requesting a favor, reminding your partner, or criticizing to evoke a change, close your mouth and breathe. Your silence will create the space for your partner to move toward you. Then when your partner moves in your

direction, respond in love and kindness, then make a note to
remember and savor it when you need it in the future.

💚 **Practice mutual accountability.** In healthy relationships
partners are responsible for the ways they create distance.
Whether it's by pursuing or distancing, it's important to
be curious and compassionate about yourself and the ways
you learned to protect yourself. It's important to remember
we are not bad people; our individual coping mechanisms
happen automatically.

The good news is, when we spend positive time together and
fill the space between us with presence, curiosity, calm voices, and
soft eyes, *we connect*. We connect and we regulate each other's
emotions in all the ways that bring us closer together.

13

Your Anxiety/Depression Is Tearing Us Apart

Your anxiety/depression is becoming increasingly hard to deal with. I know it's hard on you but it affects me too—and everyone else around you. I don't think you have any idea how exhausting it is to be constantly monitoring your emotional state and never knowing when something will send you into that place again. It takes an enormous amount of energy for me to feel normal, let alone happy, when you are depressed, angry, anxious—or all of the above!

I get it that you are in distress. On a good day I have nothing but compassion for you and tell myself you are doing the best you can. I vow not to take it personally and reassure myself that we will get through this. But the longer it goes on, the more doubtful I become. It's definitely taking a toll on our relationship.

It's particularly distressing when you blame me. You don't always come right out and say it, but you definitely send that message. In the beginning I believed you—and maybe that's still right—but I can't see a connection between my behavior and your mental state. A gesture that pleases you one day will provoke you the next; I can't predict, and I'm not a mind reader. All I know is the stress and uncertainty are building a wall between us.

The tough part is, I feel like I've lost my best friend. I can't count on you to be there for me or support me because you are so wrapped up in your own emotional world. You are not dependable as a partner; I can't even bring it up for discussion for fear you will feel worse and then blame me.

It appears to me you live more and more in an emotional state where I can no longer reach you. Is that what you want? To be away from me? At times it feels like you are trying to drive me away. Would that make you feel better if I just left?

Oh, it is so hard to see you in such misery. I want to help, but I have to accept the fact that I can't do it for you. I'm starting to feel hopeless about our relationship.

The Purpose Behind Anxiety/Depression

Twenty percent of us have experienced at least a period of depression, and about the same number have lived through a time when our lives were fraught with anxiety. When you experience one of these distressed states—and yes, they often go together—it's difficult to determine the underlying cause behind those feelings.

Even professionals are still learning about the complex causes of depression and anxiety. In most cases, these emotional states don't have a single cause. They can arise from any combination of things such as your genetic makeup, current lifestyle, health conditions, trauma, stressful events, or medication. Even habits such as drug and alcohol use, dietary choices, and your cognitive style can affect you.

When our physiology (body or psyche) is out of balance, we try to cope in the best possible way. Some of us turn our energy out by becoming chaotic or anxious; others turn energy in, becoming rigid or depressed. We even can vacillate between emotional states. Anxiety or depression can be part of your natural defense, an attempt to correct an imbalance.

Growing up, many of us didn't learn how to self-regulate effectively. It's not because we had bad parents—most parents do their best—but because of traumas such as the death of a close family member; physical or mental illness; separation or divorce; injury and accidents; unemployment/underemployment and poverty; isolation or neglect; physical violence and war; or other disasters, natural or manmade, that were overwhelming and too hard for us to handle. When adults don't regulate their own emotions in a healthy manner, children do not learn how to regulate theirs. This can go on, passed from generation to generation.

Bear in mind, the purpose behind depression/anxiety is to send a message. The content of the message may be a reflection of your physical state, your emotional state, your cognitive state, or the state of your lifestyle or relationship. No one consciously chooses anxiety or depression. They are highly stressful physiological states that erode happiness and stability.

The Disconnect from Anxiety/Depression

Emotional states are contagious, and our hardwiring for connection enables us to feel what others are feeling. For the sake of survival, it's vital to read the signals from others and respond in the best possible (and safest) way. This reading or receiving of emotions is unconscious and immediate; when one partner is depressed, the other feels depressed; when one partner is anxious, the other gets anxious, too.

It hurts to be close to someone who is in pain. It hurts for many reasons. First, we want the people we love to be happy and safe. Second, when the person we love is hurting, that pain will automatically be mirrored in us. Third, living with people who are trapped in their own anxiety/depression is exhausting. It takes energy to manage all the distress signals. It's like hearing, "Mayday! Mayday!" and not being able to help.

Anxiety and depression are associated with danger, making these emotional states particularly alarming to the nervous system—whether it's you or your partner in distress. When we detect another's suffering, defenses spring into action. We try to help, out of love and desire to relieve pain, but also because we, too, get overwhelmed by our own feelings in the presence of such pain. (You begin to get the picture of two people in pain trying to help themselves, as well as each other.) The sheer exhaustion of this experience will eventually wear you down and send you into a defensive position separated from one another, both emotionally and physically.

Transforming Anxiety/Depression

The first step in transforming anxiety or depression is to remove any blame and shame. When we remove this weight we do several things for ourselves as well as our relationships. For one, we see the big picture of how natural and human it is for all of us to experience strong anxiety, paralyzing sadness, or feelings of hopelessness and depression.

Anxiety and depression are among the top ten disabilities around the world. Millions of people suffer—and millions *recover*. Here are some suggestions for transformation.

Seek help. All forms of anxiety and depression need to be taken seriously. While we all go through stressful periods, if you have felt anxious, fearful, nervous, unusually fatigued, worthless, guilty, or a sense of foreboding for more than two weeks, that can be cause for seeking outside assistance. If you have sleep disturbance serious enough to interfere with daily functioning, or a change in your eating patterns, again, it is wise to get help from a professional.

Sometimes a little help can make a huge difference. Help can be as simple as visiting a medical doctor for a comprehensive check-up. Anxiety as well as depression can be symptoms of disease or a side effect of medication. In addition, if the anxiety or depression is to be treated with medication, in most states you will need a medical doctor to administer necessary prescriptions. If medication is the right choice for treatment, seek out a psychiatrist who can manage both your treatment and any appropriate medication. Hold on to your core values when starting any prescriptions because medications take time to be effective. A knowledgeable and reassuring physician can be vital during this process.

Psychotherapy is useful in alleviating anxiety as well as depression, especially when you put in the necessary effort. Cognitive Behavioral Therapy in particular has a strong track record of helping individuals manage their thoughts and emotions in a highly effective manner.

Treating anxiety and depression is a specialty; if you are not getting the results you need, seek a second opinion. Keep knocking on doors until you find the right path.

Make lifestyle changes. Small adjustments can make life feel so much easier. Adding moderate exercise, gardening, a hobby, mindfulness and meditation, yoga, dancing, etc., to your life can revitalize you—not to mention your relationship! A supportive partner can be an integral part of your transformation.

Let's not rule out the need for larger lifestyle adjustments. Job stress, climate effects, and financial problems can require major changes in the way you go about living. Changing jobs, moving, downsizing, or rightsizing to alleviate financial stress can provide relief if they are causing your anxious/depressed state.

Get support from others who know. Genetics can play a part in causing anxiety and depression. Talking with family members about their transformations can be helpful. Not surprisingly, a medication or therapy that works for one family member oftentimes will work for another. If nothing else, it can be helpful simply explaining to family members how they can (or maybe cannot) be helpful.

Check out self-help sources. Don't forget the commonly used resources you can find in books, tapes, and workshops.

Give yourself credit. If you are managing anxiety and/or depression just getting through each day can be a challenge. For this reason, it's important to focus on changes you have made and celebrate each step of the way. As a partner, another way you can assist is by noting and acknowledging these positive changes during transformation.

Consider couples therapy. Some relationship issues can create anxiety and depression. Living with a partner who is other than truthful; living with someone who is unavailable and focuses energy on another person, hobby, pastime, or addiction; living with a partner who is not fully committed to the relationship; and living with someone who is critical, angry, or rageful can create anxiety and/or depression. These issues are best addressed in professional counseling.

Take personal responsibility. If you are causing your partner's anxious/depressed response it's up to you to make the necessary changes to alleviate it. Again, professional help is the most efficient way to do this. If you haven't caused the angst, then it's best not to take it personally. Instead, do your best to support your partner with compassion and cooperation as you work together as a transformation team.

Anxiety and depression don't have to tear your relationship apart. Put a heart around the problem and your relationship, for compassion and kindness will guide you both through this challenging transformation.

14

Your Anger Is
Tearing Us Apart

Are you seriously still angry at me? Or are you mad about something else now? I don't understand why you are always so mad. I never know if it's something I've said or done, or maybe it's something I didn't do. I feel like whenever I open my mouth your response is always the same: You get angry.

It's almost as if the sight of my face puts you in a perpetual bad mood because you seem to get mad whenever I walk in the room. Do you even remember the last time we had a reasonable, two-way conversation? Is it even possible for us to have a conversation that doesn't end with you walking away angry and slamming doors? The tension between us is unbearable, and I feel like we're always on the brink of World War III.

We used to enjoy spending time together, hanging out, talking, and laughing. What changed? How did we end up here? What have I done wrong? I've tried everything and feel like there's nothing I can do to make you happy or to please you. I'm so sad and confused, and I feel hopeless about our future together.

The Purpose Behind Anger

Evolutionary theorists categorize anger as a negative emotion, but the biological purpose of anger makes it a positive force in our ability to survive. Anger is designed for protection and correction. As such, anger is a natural, automatic emotional response to feeling threatened. Whether the threat is real or perceived, anger sounds the alarm and mobilizes you for "fight or flight" action.

Anger also gives you a burst of energy to defend or rescue yourself or others from threat or harm.

With feelings ranging from slight annoyance to outrage and fury, anger commands immediate attention and motivates behavior. If you see a child run into a busy street, anger is often your immediate reaction. Yelling, "Get back here!" sounds the alarm and says, "Danger!" Anger gets everyone focused and alerts to signs of trouble. The surge of cortisol and adrenaline that accompanies anger can provide the strength and motivation to tackle situations you ordinarily might avoid.

Feelings of anger are normal and actually can be beneficial for identifying ways to improve your relationship. Anger often shows up when something isn't right or needs to change, essentially providing a protective barrier that says, "Back off!" Emotional triggers such as irritation, frustration, interference, disappointment, rejection, embarrassment, fear, shame, and boundary violation can fuel feelings of anger to signal something's wrong. Sometimes it can be tricky knowing exactly *what's* wrong or needs to change, especially when we use anger to avoid, cover up, or deny underlying emotional pain.

Shouting and swearing are obvious signs of anger, but your safety and survival sometimes depend on responding to nonverbal cues. Fortunately, the body's limbic system always monitors for signs of danger. This means you're constantly, without thinking about it, "reading" people's emotions through facial expressions, body language, tone of voice, and timing. Mirror neurons imitate emotions you see and sense in others. Glaring eyes, a reddened face, furrowed brow, tense jaw, clenched fists, or folded arms can warn you when someone's angry before you hear any alarming words.

An appropriate anger response is one that is equal to the threat or perceived violation. However, anger often emerges so quickly and with such intensity that it can be difficult to manage and easy to overreact. When you feel threatened, your emotional responses are automatic, not necessarily appropriate or accurate. When it comes to your well-being, your brain will err in the direction of safety even if further evidence proves it wrong. This inherent biological design comes in handy in emergencies but easily can wreck your relationship.

The Disconnect from Anger

The health and success of your relationship depends greatly on how well you and your partner manage negative emotions such as anger. Although angry actions and words can cause considerable damage, angry feelings alone don't ruin relationships—it's the *escalation* of anger that tears couples apart.

Happy, stable couples have the same number of problems as unhappy couples, but the difference is they have the skills to manage conflict and restore connection with one another. You likely know couples who fight like cats and dogs one minute, then make love the next. Anger and arguing don't predict breakups; it's the pattern of escalation and build-up of resentment, contempt, and disconnect that break you apart.

Escalation often looks like a ping-pong match, with couples serving verbal assaults back and forth trying to outmatch one another. We've all been there before—instead of listening to each other's perspective and trying to solve the problem, we focus on keeping score and planning what to say in the next attack. During the emotional mayhem we tend to say and do things we'll later regret, making it more difficult to recover, repair, and reconnect.

Escalating anger doesn't always involve lashing out with raised voices, profanity, name calling, and accusations. Shutting down, getting quiet, and stonewalling are evidence of escalation as well. That's because most attempts to evoke change manifest negatively as criticism and blame, and when you criticize, you drive your partner to disconnect and defend.

A certain amount of disclosure must take place between partners to foster feelings of intimacy and keep you connected. Both consistent and unpredictable episodes of anger create roadblocks that prevent personal sharing. "If you are going to be angry at me, I'm going to be very careful about what I say to you." When defenses are up, connection is down—and disconnection is the fast track to growing apart.

When anger generates a more intense response beyond what's appropriate for the triggering event, it is often fueled by implicit memories of past events that may have little or nothing to do with the present problem. Feelings influenced by implicit memories emerge with sensations but no recollection. Your brain tries to make sense of the situation by wrongly attributing those sensations to the present, causing an overreaction.

When you overreact, the people closest to you are the most likely targets, and inevitably that means blaming your partner: "I'm feeling anxious and it's your fault!" Your overreaction is an affront to your partner because your behavior is out of line and inappropriate for the situation. As a result, you lose your power of persuasion and drive your partner into a defensive position rather than being receptive and open to your influence and opinion.

Anger is an extremely powerful emotion that can be very scary and destructive, especially when anger is used to punish, manipulate, control, or threaten. Angry outbursts and verbal aggression can be just as intimidating and damaging as physical abuse. Your relationship should be a safe haven, but you can't feel safe in a relationship with toxic behaviors of anger. If you find yourself stuck in a toxic relationship, don't do it alone—get help immediately.

Transforming Anger

Transforming negative emotions begins with awareness and recognizing the different triggers. Once you learn to identify the triggers for anger, you can start transforming those feelings and behaviors in a constructive way. *Just because you feel angry does not mean you should always act on those feelings.* Awareness gives you an opportunity to manage your emotions and decide how you want to respond.

Recall the last time you were annoyed, mad, or even outraged. Think about it, and write down your answers to the following:

- What is causing you to feel angry?
- Is this your issue or your partner's issue?
- Does something need to change? Is it something you can change? Or is it your reaction and perspective that needs to change?
- Will change give you the result you want?

Now recall the last time your partner was irritated or angry. Think about it, and go back and write down answers to the previous questions.

We don't have much control over when we feel emotions, but we can learn how to recognize and manage them to produce more positive, productive results. Here are some tips for learning how to regulate your own emotions:

Tip 1: Don't go there. Before you let anger get the best of you, visualize a stop sign 🛑. Thought-stopping can short-circuit anger. The less angry you are, the less angry you will become.

Tip 2: Get beneath the anger. Anger is often a secondary emotion to the primary feelings of hurt, fear, or shame. Get to the source of your anger and put it into constructive action.

Tip 3: Become an expert in detecting the early warning signs of anger. Stress, lack of sleep, hunger, loneliness, too much stimulation, multi-tasking, lack of affection—all can trigger anger. Track your signs and develop a proactive plan for self-care to prevent the build-up.

Tip 4: Take responsibility for your own anger regardless of what your partner does. As long as you are blaming, you are stuck in anger.

Tip 5: Get support. If your anger feels out of control or like it's getting the best of you or your relationship, get help. Coaches, therapists, and spiritual leaders can be of great assistance in freeing you from this powerful emotion.

What makes you angry may or may not make your partner angry. Our emotional experiences—and underlying motivations—are unique. We have different ways of expressing anger, and different ways of dealing with anger from our partners. Recognizing difference in our partner helps us better understand and respect each other's reality. *You will never get your partner to care about how you feel if you don't care about how your partner feels.*

In the past you might have heard you need to get your anger out because holding it in will make you depressed. For years, mental health experts described depression as anger turned inward; we now know that anger is more often depression turned outward. Get support and get beneath your anger. Don't let your anger make you even angrier.

Recurrent anger can be a symptom of *depression*. Depression can be situational, a result of psychological factors like poor coping style or low self-esteem, or a result of your biochemistry. Whatever the cause, if you suspect depression is the underlying root of anger in your relationship, start with professional help from a medical doctor.

Anger is a numbing emotion we sometimes use to cover up unpleasant and oftentimes unbearable feelings. Women often use anger to avoid feeling loss, fear, or abandonment; men often use anger to avoid feeling shame. We also use anger as a form of punishment. Anger may extinguish immediate behavior in the moment, but it increases the probability the behavior will increase and continue later in another setting.

Men, especially, use silence and distancing as protection from underlying anger. We rely on aggressiveness for protection, and it takes a lot of energy to manage the anger that accompanies aggression. When a man distances himself, think twice before you provoke him. A man's stonewalling behavior most often is a form of protection; a woman's stonewalling behavior most often is a form of punishment.

Managing conflict is part of being in a relationship, and couples can learn how to transform anger and even disagree with one another *without* escalation. The key is recognizing the triggers and identifying the underlying motivation. Then you can take appropriate action to de-escalate an angry situation and work together to repair any damage.

15

Your Addiction
Is Tearing Us
Apart

My stomach twists in knots and I get nauseous when I come home and find you out of it—again. You are in your own world, and it's a world that doesn't include me. Do you have any idea how much you change when you get in that altered state? You become a completely different person.

I know all the signs, and I know you are at it again. Your voice changes. Your body language is different. I see the evidence even though you think I don't. I'm tired of the denial; I'm tired of living alone; I'm tired of not being able to depend on you. This is not what I signed up for.

I miss our contact. I miss our love. I miss the fun we had. I miss you, and I miss the two of us together.

You are addicted. There, I said it. I said the unspeakable "A" word. And your addiction scares me.

I'm tired of feeling like a failure where you are concerned. Am I not enough to make you stop? Is the addiction more important to you than I am? Is the addiction more important to you than the two of us and our relationship?

I don't want to hear any more excuses or any more lies. Words never change anything. You promise me you'll change but you don't. You get defensive and I get angry and nothing changes . . . like the tears I'm crying now. I feel so hopeless and helpless, and I don't know what to do next.

The Purpose Behind Addiction

Altering your state of consciousness is a common act—and we all do it. Whether it's morning coffee to wake up, an afternoon Diet Coke to re-energize, or a glass of wine to relax before bedtime, most of us use substances for attitude adjustments. We also use food for reasons other than nourishment. Who hasn't turned to a chunk of chocolate to correct the course of a crappy day, or dunked a few donuts to diminish a depressed mood?

It's one thing to use substances within a healthy framework, but another to cross the line into addiction—and it can be very difficult to see the difference.

Wanting to feel good is normal and healthy. When we are in physical or emotional pain we want relief immediately! It's only human to seek solace when your soul is suffering. And by the way, no one really knows what it's like being *you*.

When the nervous system is out of balance (it happens to all of us) we try to regulate ourselves in the best ways we know how. We turn to many substances and activities: alcohol, drugs, sex, shopping, the Internet, and gambling are just a few examples of sources we use to alter consciousness, take away pain, and get a lift—at least momentarily.

What happens after a while is we build up tolerance. One drink won't make you feel good; one pill won't do the trick. You must consume more (shopping or sipping) to feel the same effect. Before you know it you've crossed the line and can't get back.

It is important to understand that addiction has a biological as well as psychological component. Some people can manage a healthy relationship with addictive substances and activities, while others simply cannot. The key is knowing if you are a person who can have a healthy relationship, or someone who cannot.

The Disconnect from Addiction

We use addictive behaviors to feel different and to change our state or mood. Sometimes a stiff person gets friendlier or a quiet person becomes talkative. This can be quite confusing for relationships: Why are you acting so different? Are you being friendly or is it the addiction that's being friendly? Will the real you stand up?

When you are in an altered state you become very self-centered. Frequently, the addictive habit becomes your primary relationship. Addiction is all-consuming, and it takes over your life. You may love your partner deeply, but your focus is on the addiction, not connection. When an addiction becomes your partner, you've actually left the relationship.

More often than not, an altered state ultimately takes a negative toll on your relationship, primarily because your partner becomes a competitor to the addiction for time and attention. An addicted brain will choose the substance over sustaining the relationship.

If the partner takes on the task of managing the addiction, this begins a losing battle, which can go on indefinitely with a very sad outcome. Neither person is happy, and the relationship suffers.

Transforming Addiction

First we need to look at addiction without shame. Shame can get in the way of responsibility and change. Being kidnapped by an addiction doesn't make you a bad person. What's important to understand is the addiction can take control, and willpower alone rarely can stop you or make you change.

Second, *put a heart around* both partners as well as the addiction. If your partner thinks you have an addiction—be curious and open to it; consider the possibility. Understand that holding you accountable for personal actions that affect the relationship is most often an act of love. Wanting you to be more present as opposed to being in an altered state and self-focused, is a normal desire from a partner.

If you are the one using or abusing, put a heart around yourself and understand you share not only addiction, but recovery, with millions of other people. It can happen to anybody.

If you live with an addicted person, focus attention on yourself about how you can be stronger, happier and calmer—regardless of what your partner does.

Next, let's look at the common line between use and abuse. Regarding the substance use, consider these questions:

- ♥ Have you experienced an irresistible urge to use against your conscious wishes?
- ♥ Do you anticipate and dwell on the use beforehand?
- ♥ Have you made promises or plans to cut back or quit but eventually went back to old patterns?
- ♥ Do you have the sense that you are not in complete control of the use?
- ♥ Are you spending increasing time in an altered state?
- ♥ When you are not using, are you thinking about using?
- ♥ Have you lied to yourself or others about your use?
- ♥ Are you in denial about the money you are spending?

♥ Have you missed commitments or declined important invitations because of your use?

♥ Are you using more now than you did in the beginning?

♥ Do you feel guilt, shame, or embarrassment about your use?

♥ Are the people who love you concerned about your use?

Answering "yes" to even a few of these questions can be cause for alarm and a signal to seek help. If your best thinking got you to the point of answering in the affirmative to three or more of these questions, then you might need to seek help from an expert.

God, grant me the serenity to accept the things I cannot change,
The courage to change the things I can,
And the wisdom to know the difference.

The Twelve-Step Program Serenity Prayer highlights the most important challenges for overcoming an addiction: 1) you must be rigorously honest about your addiction, and 2) you must take ownership and take control. These challenges are not easy because honesty can trigger shame. Shame is a very difficult feeling to bear; nobody likes feeling ashamed. Shame often sets off denial, and denial masks the shame of knowing you are out of control. Answering the questions about use versus abuse can help you break through denial and illuminate the seriousness of the issue.

Remember, *addiction is the addict's responsibility.* Your partner doesn't cause your addiction, and your partner can't fix it! As partners in a relationship, you both have your own work to do. Fortunately, there are numerous resources available when you need outside help.

16

Your Affair
Is Tearing Us
Apart

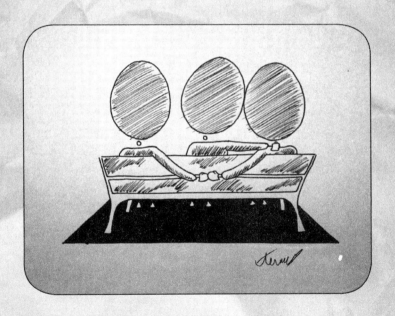

Just the thought of you with someone else literally makes me feel sick. Right now as the picture comes into my mind, I feel a churning in my stomach and tightness in my throat threatening to choke me.

I can't believe you would do this to me. I can't believe you would do this to us! After all we have gone through and after all we have built together, I can't believe you would throw it all away without a thought or concern for anyone but yourself.

What were you thinking? Did you even think of how I would feel? Did you even care? Do you care now? And what about our family? Does this stranger mean more to you than your own family? Is your pleasure worth tearing this whole family apart? You have ruined all our lives just to follow your feelings and please yourself.

So is this about sex? Are you not attracted to me anymore? Did you ever find me attractive? Am I such a miserable failure? It feels like my heart is being torn out of my body. Why are you doing this to me? Why?

I don't think you have any idea how much this hurts me. Yes, I've been angry—I'm still angry! But I am also deeply sad. I'm grieving the loss of a dream; I guess it was a dream because I thought we had a strong, loving relationship, while all along you were giving your love and attention secretly to someone else.

How could you look at me and act like nothing was happening while knowing you were lying to my face? Some part of me feels like a big fool—for loving you, believing you, and trusting you. Well, you've broken that trust, and I don't know if I can ever get that back again.

The Purpose Behind Affairs

People have affairs for a variety of reasons, but the ones cited most often are "It feels good," and "It's fun." Although most of us enjoy the security, companionship, and comfort of a committed, monogamous relationship, we also might desire the passion and intensity that comes from a new relationship, especially a secret one.

People have affairs because they consider it nobody else's business (not even their partners'). The affair might just be about sex; it could be an emotional affair they don't consider infidelity; it might add spice to their committed relationship; it might be a lifelong personal style and they have no interest in changing; it might awaken a part of their personality lying dormant for years; they may feel entitled to the affair, a reward for working hard and fulfilling responsibilities. An affair can also be payback or a passive-aggressive act against the committed partner.

Most people, however, don't decide—they *slide* into an affair. Conscious thought doesn't enter into the picture. An innocent acquaintance gradually becomes more intimate until it's the primary source of pleasure. The affair begins with two people sharing information or an activity; they bond around personal contact and mutual experiences. With little or no conscious thought, they cross the line into infatuation. The critical point is when the original purpose for that relationship changes: when the focus of the relationship changes from business to pleasure or from friendship to romantic intimacy; when contact is made to engage the other person intimately and not to get the workplace job done.

Once the affair relationship starts to provide a sensual or sexual high, then it's "game over." You are now under the influence of infatuation, one of the strongest forces found in nature. Infatuation sets up an insatiable craving for more contact that's practically impossible to resist. The easiest time to end an affair is long before infatuation begins.

It's easy to be judgmental about affairs, but in fairness, being attracted to another person is normal. Even falling in love with another person is normal. Monogamy *isn't* normal. Non-monogamy *isn't* normal either. What's normal is *variety*.

We are innately designed to do relationships a lot of different ways. Some people come genetically programmed for monogamy, and it's their natural state. For these partners, it takes little effort to maintain monogamy once they form an attachment bond. This doesn't mean they can't or won't be unfaithful or non-monogamous; it's just that monogamy is easier.

Another group of people come genetically programmed in a way that makes monogamy feel less natural. It's not that they can't be monogamous, but it just takes more conscious effort.

Some couples choose to take the non-monogamous route to relationships. They make a mutually agreed-upon plan to include other people in their love life. Infidelity is when another partner is included *without* mutual consent.

An important clarification regarding affairs—contrary to popular belief—is that affairs can and do happen in good relationships. The reason is because infidelity has a lot to do with proximity. You can be in a happily committed relationship and still meet someone at work with whom you have chemistry. If you follow the chemistry very far, an affair is in your future.

Just as there are many reasons why affairs happen, there are many ways to be unfaithful. You can betray by sharing emotions, sexuality, finances, loyalty, as well as time and attention, with any number of others at the expense of the relationship. You can have an emotional affair with a child; a loyalty affair with work; a time-stealing affair with friends—all for the same reasons: it feels good and it's enjoyable.

The Disconnect from Affairs

Infidelity threatens the connection between two people in many ways. Affairs break trust, lack of trust creates anxiety, and managing anxiety is exhausting. Affair-repair takes a lot of energy and how many of us have energy to spare these days?

Affairs change your image of your partner. Whether you had the affair or you're reeling from your partner's affair, the experience will show you another side of one another's personality. Recovering from an affair can bring out the best in us, but oftentimes it brings out the worst. When we are in the throes of fear or shame, none of us function at our best. These experiences are hard to forget and become part of the legacy of your relationship.

Affairs are traumatic. Trauma is any real or perceived threat to survival. When you are in a committed love relationship your partner becomes an attachment figure. This means, in the most primitive part of your brain (the part that is in charge of your survival), your partner's attention determines whether you live or die. So if your partner chooses someone else over you, it feels like you are going to die. This traumatic experience creates a myriad of feelings, from agony to ecstasy, and you can shift from one extreme to another in the blink of an eye.

Affairs evoke fear of abandonment. Being excluded, left out, or abandoned is the worst fear for many, and when someone does this *to you* it's very difficult not to take it personally. Even though affairs most often are the result of your partner's unilateral, personal decision, it's hard not to take it (at least initially) as a personal affront. When you're reeling in the hurt it's hard to reach the love that once connected you.

Affairs evoke shame in several ways, and either partner can feel shame. For example, the unfaithful partner can feel shame because:

- ♥ I broke my promise of fidelity. I lied and cheated.

- ♥ I gave away what I promised to you.

- ♥ I went against my core values. I disappointed the people I love.

- ♥ I lied to my affair partner and to my committed partner.

The betrayed partner can feel shame because:

- ♥ I did my best to hurt you because you hurt me.

- ♥ I told other people what you did to punish you.

- ♥ Like a fool, I trusted you.

- ♥ I took you back after all the hurt, the betrayal, and everything you've done.

- ♥ I'll put up with anything, so what does that say about me?

Shame is a disabling feeling that can make you want to hide, shut down, and disconnect from the pain as well as the partner.

Affairs cause pain for everyone involved. Pain makes us defend and protect ourselves. You don't feel connected when you're busy defending.

Transforming Affairs

Affairs can bring about the best and worst of times for the two people trying to repair their relationship. The best of times can include having great sex, feeling romantic love again, realizing how important you are to one another, having fun together, laughing, being affectionate, crying together, making new commitments, being vulnerable and compassionate—yes this happens to couples while they are struggling to recover from infidelity. Many people even lose weight and get more physically fit.

Affairs can also bring about the worst of times. If you had the affair you may feel like you never loved your committed partner in the first place. You may grieve the loss of the affair partner and resent your committed partner for taking that away. You might believe you'll never be as happy as you were with the affair partner. You might even believe you have lost the love of your life.

If you are the betrayed partner, you may feel like you're riding an emotional roller coaster. You may feel like your whole life has been a lie and the rug was pulled out from under you. You may have feelings of hatred and revenge, even violence—something you never thought you could feel. You may hear words coming out of your mouth that would embarrass George Carlin. You may become obsessed about micromanaging your partner's behavior and want to monitor every hour of the day. You may hack a phone or computer, plant a GPS device, or hire a private detective. You may want to stay one minute and run away forever in the next.

Or, you might both take the affair in stride and move on with little or no consequence.

The reason we list these behaviors is to emphasize they are all normal. As crazy as they may seem at the time, for the most part, this is temporary insanity. The good news is, it's not only possible to survive but to thrive in a relationship after an affair. Here are some basic steps to facilitate the process:

Step One—ZERO Contact: Generally, recovery and repair can't begin until there is zero contact with the affair partner. That means no face-to-face visits, phone calls, emails, texts, or Internet contact—nothing. That also means no pining, fantasizing, re-reading communications, listening to your "special music," or revisiting the love scenes. This can be especially difficult when the affair involves someone from work.

Step Two—Informed Consent: Most individuals need some relevant information and facts about the betrayal including, but not limited to, names, places, time spent together, money spent on affair/affair partner, activities, and details. The partner who was betrayed has the right to the information to make an informed decision about moving forward. It's difficult to rebuild a relationship without a foundation of honesty. Giving relevant information is also an indication that the unfaithful partner is protecting the committed partner not the affair partner.

Step Three—Remorse: The partner who betrayed must understand and have compassion for the betrayed partner's pain caused by the infidelity. This is a pivotal step. Without remorse, forgiveness is difficult, if not impossible. Without remorse, further betrayal is probable.

Step Four—Building Trust: Say what you are going to do. Do it. Then repeat the process. This takes time and is a difficult period for both parties. The first year is the "year of the firsts." This is my first birthday knowing about the affair. Where were you on my birthday last year?

Step Five—Forgiveness: This step is vital for the relationship to grow and prosper, and it is often a difficult process for the betrayed partner.

Step Six—Create a New Contract: This doesn't mean you need a formal, legal document (although this isn't as uncommon as you might think), but be sure you're in agreement about what it means to be in a committed, monogamous relationship. Most couples commit to being lovers, best friends, confidants, playmates, financial partners, social partners, each other's priority above everything else, and always on each other's side.

Recommitment. Most couples get into relationships without discussing expectations and behaviors that are acceptable and unacceptable for the relationship. It's important for both of you to be on the same page about your recommitment to one another.

Some couples even have a recommitment ceremony after a period of healing and forgiveness.

After the affair. Once time has passed and healing has begun it may be important to look at issues that were in play before the affair took place. Addressing unresolved issues, changing communication patterns, and revitalizing your sex life may be in order as you move forward together, but only well after you both have recovered from the betrayal.

The ultimate question for couples facing infidelity is this: what kind of person do you want to be? Consider these questions to formulate your answer:

- ♥ What kind of man do you want to be?
- ♥ What kind of woman do you want to be?
- ♥ What are your core values?
- ♥ How can you live each day with authenticity and without regret?

Recovering from an affair can be well worth the hard work. Many couples will tell you even though they never would have chosen this path, their relationship became stronger and more rewarding through the journey.

17

Your Selfishness Is Tearing Us Apart

At times I am just incredulous at how selfish you are! I can't believe that you're not embarrassed by your behavior. I wish I had a videotape of you going through the day. You must say the word "I" thousands of times. Why can't you just shut up and listen once in a while and be curious about someone else for a change? Get out of your own frame of reference? Furthermore, when was the last time you went out of your way to help me? To think of me and put me first? When you need me, I'm expected to drop everything and tend to your wishes, but when I need you it's like I am nothing but an inconvenience.

It's not just your conversations; your time, attention, and interest all lead to the same place: you. Oh, I know you are going to say how hard you work and how much you do, but I work too—although you rarely notice or appreciate it. The way I see it, any effort you exert ultimately benefits you the most or you don't do it at all. If you look at the bottom line, most of what you do is about pleasing yourself.

Life isn't all about you. It's not just about what you want, what happened to you, or how I and others don't meet your expectations. I get so tired of hearing about your needs, your feelings, your opinions, and whatever you think is important! I know this sounds mean, like I'm beating you up with my words, but how else am I going to get my point across? I hate having to get angry to get your attention, but nothing else works.

This one-dimensional life with you at the center is getting more and more difficult to tolerate. How can I respect or even like you when you are so self-absorbed and self-centered? How can I continue to love someone who rarely thinks of me in a generous or thoughtful way?

To be honest, I have a hard time finding evidence that you think of my needs at all. If I ignored you the way you ignored me, or if I spent my time, money, and energy on myself without any thought for you, then either I'd never hear the last of it or you'd be gone.

I feel like an idiot for caring for someone who cares so little for me. I keep waiting for you to reach out and show interest in me, or suggest an activity that I might enjoy, but I'm losing hope. It seems to me that in your world love is a one-way street and all roads lead to you!

The Purpose Behind Selfishness

From the moment of birth our survival depends on our ability to be seen, heard, cared for, and understood. This dependency and desire for attention lingers well into adulthood, where being ignored can still feel life-threatening. Humans are hard-wired for connection, and we experience pain each and every time we don't get it.

While growing up, if your needs were met more often than not, and if you experienced logical limits and delayed gratification, then you learned how to calm yourself and have compassion for others in distress. However, if you lived with neglect, never knowing if your needs would be met, then demanding attention at all times feels like a smart strategy. Or, if you had a caregiver (or even a partner) who made you the center of attention, who placed your whims, wants, and wishes over anyone else's, then you might assume this is the way the world works: *others exist to make me happy.*

To be seen and understood is a human need. When you don't get meaningful contact, you experience an emotional pain that can kidnap your attention and blind you to the needs of others. When you experience physical pain, it's almost impossible to focus on anything else but getting relief. Emotional pain works the same way. Oftentimes, what looks like selfishness, self-focus, or ego is really a cry for help.

The Disconnect from Selfishness

Connection occurs when two separate individuals are joined by the mutual experience of tuning in and responding to one another. This attunement requires differentiation, which means calmly holding on to your own uniqueness while acknowledging the presence and uniqueness of your partner. When both partners are differentiated, you can feel calm and composed when the two of you are close or distant, when you agree or disagree, and when you give or receive attention.

The most memorable, intimate connections occur when partners support and respond to one another: *I am here for you, and you are here for me, in our own inimitable ways.* Together, you are two separate individuals who are connected by communication; you hear each other's signals and respond appropriately to one another. The magic of intimacy materializes when *I tune in to you and you tune in to me, in spontaneous, reciprocal ways.*

The key to connection is finding pleasure in giving *and* receiving. Hyper-focusing on your own needs prevents intimacy because intimate connection requires mutual participation. Intimacy can't happen when: *I am doing my part by tuning in to your needs, but you are focused only on yourself. If you don't respond to me in the same manner, then you are only receiving, not giving.* The intimacy of connection requires both giving and receiving from each partner. You begin to see how one selfish partner can derail a relationship.

Imagine what it's like living with someone who always expects to receive love and attention but rarely is willing to give it back. Self-focused individuals *expect* their desires to be a priority, but this one-way approach makes it almost impossible for generosity because giving is already expected. Expectancy deprives both partners from the joys of generosity, gratitude, and thoughtfulness.

Relationship happiness comes not just from being loved, but from *loving*. The self-focused partner will be limited in relationship if the focus is always about receiving but never giving. The relationship will wither from lack of connection.

The pain of disconnection can create a negative spiral in a relationship. None of us is at our best when in pain. When one partner is so self-focused, unable to tune in, and only interested in receiving and never giving, then the relationship consists of two partners in pain, simply trying to cope and rarely able to connect. Disconnection rips at the seams, slowly tearing relationships apart.

Transforming Selfishness

Selfishness is a tough nut to crack because most of us don't have much incentive for giving up a long-held practice that works in our favor. Old patterns are difficult to break. There is hope, however, and it lies in creating a new, more magnificent experience through *core value living*. Here's how it works:

- As a couple, refer to "Core Value Living" in Chapter 21 and complete the exercise for determining your core values. Each of you list at least three of your own core values on separate pieces of paper.

- Once you have listed three core values each, exchange papers.

- With the list in front of you, take time to think of examples from real life when you witnessed your partner demonstrating each core value. For example:

  You were generous when you gave me all your airline miles from work travel so I could visit my college roommate.

  You were dependable when you picked me up from the airport at 2:00 AM even though you had that big project at work the next day.

  You were loving when you created that romantic dinner for me on my birthday.

  You were compassionate when you took our dog to the vet when you knew I couldn't do it.

If you want to make a change, it's easier to add something positive than to eliminate something negative. Catching your partner in the act of doing something right (acting out core values) will increase the probability your partner will repeat the behavior. Living an authentic life in line with your highest and best values will generate such joy that selfishness will pale in comparison.

Selfishness, ego, or self-focus—whatever you name it—creates such a narrow view of life. If this has been your perspective, even if your partner is the only one who believes it's your perspective, then take the first step into another point of view: through your partner's world. You might begin by answering these questions:

♥ What does my partner want and need the most from me?

♥ What touches my partner's heart?

♥ What is it that I do that makes my partner happiest?

♥ Knowing my partner as I do, how can I make our relationship more meaningful?

♥ What can I give my partner that no one else can give?

Answering these questions will help you begin to enter your partner's world by way of generous giving. Notice how it feels, what it means to you, and the effect it has on you. Focus on the experience of *giving* rather than what your partner gives back in return.

Once you taste the joy of true giving, transformation begins. Meeting another's needs, making someone happy, sacrificing to please your partner—all come with intrinsic reward. If you know the longing of your partner's heart, let today be the day to fulfill that longing.

On the other hand, if you've been in relationship with someone who is more self-focused, then you may have to be clear about what you want and need. Specificity and strength are important, for example:

♥ What I want from you is . . . and an example of this would be . . .

♥ It is important to me for you to . . .

♥ What I need from you on a daily basis is . . .

♥ I feel connected to you when you . . .

♥ I feel important to you when you . . .

♥ It tells me you are thinking of me when you . . .

♥ Instead of . . . I'd like you to . . .

♥ It makes me feel like a priority when you . . .

The competitive nature of our world today may require more self-focus than ever before—but relationships do not. The path to connection runs to and from one heart to another; it's a continuous loop that takes you deeper into intimacy and love.

18

Your Communication Style Is Tearing Us Apart

There are several ways communication styles can tear your relationship apart. Here are common scenarios:

We can't have a civil conversation anymore. The simplest subject results in a verbal assault. No matter what I try, nothing seems to work. I feel like you have turned me into the enemy or someone out to get you. How are we going to maintain our relationship when there is no communication? You are like an argument waiting to happen.

You have successfully managed to shut me out. I'm your partner; I have a right to know what's going on. Anytime I approach you or simply open my mouth your response tells me you are not interested. And it's not just our conversations—or lack of them, it's also your behavior. You can reject me without saying a word.

You just don't know when to shut up. Why must you talk everything to death? It's the same issues over and over; nothing ever gets resolved. I listen and listen, but nothing changes. I think we've come to an agreement but the next thing I know you are bringing it up again for a rehash. You don't want a conversation; you want an audience—or maybe a whipping post. I'm worn out; where do I go to turn myself in?

There's an elephant in our living room. You know, that relationship-threatening issue we never talk about. We've become experts at polite avoiding, but the more we ignore it the more distant we become. I don't feel close to you anymore, and my fear is if we don't address this and get some resolution, it will tear us apart.

Your idea of communication is pout and punish. Why don't you just speak up when you are unhappy? I would rather have your words than your stone-cold wrath.

What you call communication is really capitulation. In your mind we have not "communicated" unless I agree with you. Even the tiniest decision I make can set you complaining and correcting, and spoil any part of the day. In your mind you are the communication expert . . . uh, I don't think so.

There are so many important issues that just keep coming up but never get resolved. How long can we go on like this? We might as well have two separate homes because more and more we have two separate lives.

You are so negative; your first response to anything is, "No!" Try to recall the last time we had a positive conversation, when we talked about plans for the future, or how good our life is. It's been so long since you gave me a compliment or we agreed with one another. At times it gets so antagonistic it feels like you don't even like me, let alone love me. I'm on your side but your communication style sure makes it hard to believe you are on mine.

I feel isolated and distant when you don't communicate, and trust is becoming more difficult. Furthermore, it's not just about talking; your actions sometimes speak louder than any words. Your behavior is building a barrier instead of a bridge.

You don't understand me or even make an attempt to see my point of view. You have no idea what it's like living with you. For me, communication is a key to a happy relationship—and I'm not happy.

The Purpose Behind Communication Style

Communication is a way to make yourself known in the world, and we learn different strategies very early in life. A person's communication style, therefore, is a reflection of the past as well as the present.

In a relationship, the patterns that develop are the result of two individual styles adapting to experiences within that relationship. Some communication styles we bring to the relationship, and others we develop as a result of the relationship. We impact one another, and we shape each other's responses and overtures.

One of the most confusing aspects of communication is how it can change over the course of time. The difference can be so drastic, in fact, it can feel almost like a bait-and-switch game. Communication flows freely during the initial romantic love stage. We talk, listen, share information, show interest, remember details, express affection, and long for more contact. Also called infatuation, this first stage is marked by unequivocal positive exchanges. However, infatuation is called a *stage* of love for a reason: it's time limited. Eventually, we all go back to our former lifestyles, including our communication styles. Sometimes it works—sometimes it doesn't.

The introvert/extrovert dilemma. We all fall somewhere on the introvert/extrovert continuum. Some of us naturally get more emotional and physical energy from being alone (the introvert), and others get more energy from being involved with other people (the extrovert). Yes, this is a simplification. We all are capable of using and enjoying both styles, but we do have a preference and a natural way of being in the world that's driven by DNA.

Extroverts tend to get gratification from activities outside their own minds. They need consistent human interaction and tend to be more talkative and outgoing. Extroverts are the ones who usually thrive at parties, community activities, family gatherings, and group settings. Extroverts can enjoy limited time alone but find less reward in solitary moments and easily can get bored.

Introverts get energized by quiet, contemplative time alone, and their energy quickly dissipates in large groups or boisterous situations. Introverts also like to think and examine before talking. Therefore, communication naturally moves at a slower pace—which can be problematic with an extroverted partner who tends to think out loud and "shoots from the lip."

What you're arguing about is not what you're arguing about. When big issues go unresolved there are no small issues. Even small disappointments remind you of the larger dissatisfaction. If your sexual needs have been ignored, then it's more difficult to be super thoughtful of your partner's needs. If all the housework has been left for you to manage, then the least little irritation can erupt like a volcano. Unsettled concerns often make smooth communication nigh onto impossible.

Action and reaction. If your partner is prone to criticizing, finding fault, looking on the dark side, or living in fear, then it might make sense at some level to withhold information. If the only way your partner will get off your back and quit nagging is to use your anger as a defense, then it's likely you'll take that option. If you feel like your partner never listens, then repeating yourself might get your point across. If you aren't good with words, especially when put on the spot, then going silent and withdrawing might be your best course of action. Sometimes communication style is a defensive strategy.

When talking doesn't help. If conversations consistently end in arguments; if talking never leads to positive behavior change; if you feel worse not better after a discussion—then continuing the same type of communication makes no sense.

Ignoring is more hurtful than arguing. To those of us who fear isolation, deprivation, or abandonment, being ignored is the ultimate hurt, therefore an argument or inane conversation can feel like an improvement. Having contact, even though it may lack quality, feels better than nothing at all.

A myriad of other reasons may explain why we choose a particular communication style at any given moment. What's important to remember is: we all have a need for contact, understanding, and response. The style you choose does have a purpose behind it regardless of how effective it might be.

The Disconnect
from Communication Style

Many couples who divorce or separate cite lack of communication as the cause—and this makes sense. Without contact, a way to make your needs known, and a bridge across the natural gap between two separate individuals, no relationship exists. All you have is two people going about their lives in a unilateral fashion; there's no relating in the relationship.

When communication takes so much energy and effort, there's precious little left for the good times. When you have failed at communication time and again, it's easy to give up hope and withdraw into your own shell or turn to others for support. We all need the satisfaction, support, confidence, and confirmation that effective communication gives us.

Even though couples say they can't communicate, it's impossible *not* to communicate. Walking away, shutting down, getting angry, and criticizing are all forms of communication. What couples really want is *effective* forms of communication. We want ways to relay information to one another that lead to satisfaction, joy, and fulfillment of our desires. Communication gone awry leads to heartache instead of happiness.

Communication is the way we relate our needs and learn to understand one another. Imagine trying to reach a destination without a map or a clue to guide you. That's what it's like trying to be in a relationship without a means to relay your wants and desires.

Effective communication builds trust. You can't have trust without effective communication. A relationship without trust consists of two defended partners using a lot of energy trying to protect themselves. Lack of trust brings out the worst in most of us.

Effective communication resolves conflict and misunderstandings that can otherwise build resentment and replace loving with longing. When you're lousy at communicating it increases your vulnerability to growing apart.

Transforming
Your Communication Style

Communicating your thoughts, needs, and desires with your partner will help you get what you want from the relationship, as well as help you understand your partner's point of view and draw you closer together. Sharing at a personal level also paves a fast track to intimacy and connection.

Here are several tips for transforming your communication style. Choose the tips that work best for you and your relationship.

- ♥ If you are better at listening—*talk more.*
- ♥ If you are better at talking—*listen more.*
- ♥ In important conversations, occasionally repeat what your partner says to make sure you heard correctly and to show that you are listening: "Let me see if I heard you correctly. You're saying . . ."
- ♥ Address one topic at a time. Finish one conversation before you begin another.
- ♥ Stay in the present as much as possible. Bringing up the past can create a sense of hopelessness and feeling overwhelmed.
- ♥ Pay attention to body language.
- ♥ Pick the right time for serious discussion.
- ♥ Limit the time for difficult conversations and stick to your limits.
- ♥ Use "I" statements instead of "You" statements. For example:
  - **Try saying:** *"I would love it if you told me what I was doing right more often."*
  - **Instead of:** *"You always criticize me."* No one can listen effectively when being blamed or attacked.
- ♥ Increase the probability of success by telling your partner *what* you want versus what you *don't* want. For example:
  - **Try saying:** *"I'd like some of your undivided attention as soon as possible."*
  - **Instead of:** *"Quit ignoring me."*

♥ Use the "sandwich approach" with difficult subjects. You don't have to use this approach with every paragraph you utter but begin and end any important conversation session with appreciations. For example:

- **Begin with appreciation:** *"Thank you for taking the time to talk; it means a lot to me when you make our relationship a priority."*
- **State any concern:** *"I was disappointed when you missed dinner again last night. I'd like you to make sure you are home to eat together at least four nights a week."*
- **End with more appreciation:** *"I really enjoyed our dinner Tuesday night; I actually slept better because I felt so connected to you."*

♥ When in doubt, ask your partner, "What can I do to improve our communication?" Be willing to give any suggestion a try.

If you are prone to criticizing, replace criticism with asking for what you want. Be specific and state the request positively, such as: "I would like you to have sex with me sometime in the next two days." Show appreciation when your partner pleases you or grants your request.

If you are prone to using anger in your communication style, call "time out" to calm down. Give a heartfelt apology if and when you lose it; apologizing in words will *decrease* the probability of responding in anger again in the future.

If you tend to get defensive when communicating, acknowledge it: "Hold on, I need to change the way we are talking so I can be open, not defensive." This strategy will provide an opportunity for both of you to change the manner in which you are relating to one another. It also shows goodwill and a positive intention.

If you are the one who shuts down or withdraws, the one who goes silent or seethes inside while withholding information, then do something different! For example, ask your partner: "How can I help?" "What's one small thing I can do in this moment to make things better between us?" You don't have to wait until you're in a bad place. Make it a habit to check in with your partner on a regular basis: "What can I do to help?" "What's on your mind?" "What's going on with you?" You also can ask for what you want: "Give me some time to finish reading." "Please help me with this and then we can talk later."

An important note: if one or both of you is unable or unwilling to manage and regulate your emotions and reactivity, communication always will be more difficult. The first order of business might be to seek assistance for developing skills and strategies for staying present, attuned, and on an even keel during important times of communication.

Get some coaching. It's no crime to lack relationship skills, but it is unjust to refuse help when so much good help is available. Use a therapist, take a class or workshop, read a book, go online, or download an app.

19

Your Overfunctioning, Micromanaging Behavior Is Tearing Us Apart

It's not that I don't appreciate the good things that you do for me, but sometimes I think your "helping" is really a way of micromanaging my life. When you overfunction, when you do something for me that I can do for myself, you are compensating for me—which says you think I am inadequate. No wonder you think you have to fix me. At times it seems like your whole life centers around fixing me.

When you give unsolicited advice I feel like you don't trust me to act on my own. I feel like you don't respect my intelligence. In fact, I feel like you don't respect me, period. You scrutinize my every behavior then wonder why I don't tell you things. Why should I tell you anything when your response is always the same? You'll tell me how I could have done it better and how much I hurt or upset you. Nothing I do is ever good enough for you unless I do it your way.

I know I'm going to regret being this honest with you. You act so disappointed, hurt, or angry when I express my opinion or make a choice you don't agree with. I am so tired of being responsible for your happiness and unhappiness. It's not that I don't want you to be happy, but I think your happiness is your responsibility. I wish you would focus more on yourself instead of me. Living your life through me is suffocating; it makes me want to stay away from you.

I'm grateful for many things you do, but you go overboard. You get involved where you are not invited. You do too much, then you resent it. It's like I owe you for what I didn't ask for. I know this sounds harsh and you are going to be hurt but please, please back off!

*Please quit trying to change me and instead try focusing on
yourself. Just once I'd like to hear you say what you did wrong or how
you overstepped your boundaries. I understand you want to help;
I understand your need to be involved. What I don't understand is
the compulsive need to do it all the time. Why don't you focus on your
own issues instead of mine?*

The Purpose Behind
Overfunctioning and Micromanaging

Some of us learned early in life: "There's nobody else to help
me, so if I want to get anything done I have to do it myself."
Learned at a young age, this realization can establish a reinforced
pattern of behavior that's difficult to change. Let's face it, being
able to get things done is a valuable skill, and people are rewarded
well for it throughout life. When looking for a mate, it's impressive
when you meet a take-charge, go-getter type person.

Self-sufficiency and always being the one in charge comes with
liabilities, especially when it starts at a young age. After all, there's
a lot to learn about life and its challenges. This responsibility
causes enormous anxiety. A child in charge is an anxious child,
and an anxious child manages the anxiety by doing more and
helping more. If you're this type of self-reliant person, over time,
others begin to rely on you to do more, and you feel more secure
in the relationship when you are needed. Likewise, when others
approve of you, then you can be happy. Your happiness becomes
dependent upon others.

This *quid pro quo*—giving service in exchange for love—creates
a false sense of security: "What if I don't perform?" "What if I

need help instead of provide help?" "How can I feel safe when history says there's no one there and the only true sense of safety is taking care of everything myself?" This ongoing insecurity feeds a vicious cycle of helping, then hurting, then helping more to avoid the hurt.

Adults, too, can learn these lessons and form these habits. Any crisis can change the behavior of those involved. Sometimes, couples start out and go for years with trust in place. Then a betrayal, trauma, or major shift throws one person into overdrive, and that partner becomes über responsible for the relationship.

We all have the innate need for connection and to feel safe. Helping is a way of connecting to another person, but it also can be a way of calming your nervous system.

The Disconnect from Overfunctioning and Micromanaging

We each bring our own personal issues and responsibilities to a relationship, which we can designate as "your business" and "my business." Individual boundaries and respective responsibilities separate your business from my business. For example, we are each responsible for our own personal style of dress. What you wear is *your* business; what I wear is *my* business. It's not that we don't have preferences (I have to look at you—and vice versa), but respect for your personal boundary keeps me from trying to run your business by telling you what to wear and how to wear it.

Boundaries aren't meant to be rigid, and flexibility is important. If you became very ill and unable to take care of your hygiene, then as your partner, crossing your personal boundary would be appropriate. Giving you a bath, brushing your teeth, fixing your hair, and helping you get dressed would be acts of love and compassion. Contrarily, if I crossed your personal boundary without need or invitation, my behavior would be offensive, intrusive, and a violation of your space. This situation would cause you to defend yourself. People don't feel connected when they have to defend themselves.

Boundaries aren't meant to be diffuse either. If you let me over-function and micromanage your personal hygiene by telling you when to shower, how to brush your teeth, or what to wear—when you are perfectly capable and prefer doing it yourself—then you have let your boundaries become diffuse. If this continues, you will resent me and lose respect for yourself, and ultimately we will feel more disconnected.

We have emotional boundaries in addition to physical ones. While it's important we each take personal responsibility for our own emotional well-being, certain times call for crossing emotional boundaries. For example, if you and I are in a relationship and you have had a bad day, it makes sense for me to provide comfort and support to help relieve your stress. In a sense, you "borrow" my nervous system for a period of time to calm your own. This is a good example of appropriately crossing an emotional boundary because it happens with mutual agreement and respect.

If, however, I interpret your feelings or give you unsolicited advice, then it's inappropriate and a violation of your emotional boundary. Boundary violations cause defensiveness, and defensiveness causes disconnection.

Connection occurs when two people acknowledge and respect one another's individual boundaries and willingly join together. Conscious, mutual choices promote healthy boundaries. Honoring one another's boundaries is a prerequisite for intimate connection. Relationships without connection are at great risk of tearing apart.

Transforming Overfunctioning and Micromanaging Behavior

Overfunctioning and micromanaging are intended to be helpful for both partners. (I help you and calm my nervous system at the same time.) Transformation begins by putting a heart around these behaviors and making the choice to give your partner the benefit of the doubt. Looking at any behavior through the lens of love and compassion will help you stay connected and stave off defensiveness.

The next step in transformation involves shifting your perception and creating a new process. Overfunctioning is a collaborative process, not an individual one. When your partner crosses your personal boundaries, you *allow* that to happen. As partners, you both need to create a new process:

- ♥ Set aside ten to fifteen minutes for a strategy session. Schedule the time and stick to it. Honoring time boundaries is a good step toward transformation. Having a short session also will make future strategy sessions a lot more pleasant.

- ♥ In the strategy session, think of kind and benign ways to signal when someone overfunctions, such as a smile and raised pinkie finger, or a smile and tilt of the head. Pick a signal you both agree on. The intent is for the partner who feels the invasion to say, "Stop here," in a kind way.

♥ At the signal, the overfunctioning partner says, "Thank you," and redirects the action. **Once the signal is sent and the receiving partner acknowledges with a thank-you, no further talking is allowed.**

♥ Any further discussion requires another agreed-upon strategy session at a later time. Back-to-back sessions are not recommended.

For the person who overfunctions:

♥ When you get the kind and benign signal from your partner; when you realize you have overfunctioned; or when you get the urge to micromanage, turn your focus away from your partner and toward yourself.

♥ Observe your thoughts, feelings, and especially your body sensations—tuning in to your body is essential for healing.

♥ Let any sensations flow through your body without fear of fear itself. This may sound a bit strange because we do so many things to avoid fear or pain, but when we avoid we make the feelings stronger. Instead, say to your fear: *Bring it on!* You will not die from this fear even though it feels like it. Name it to tame it: *Come on, fear, I can take it!*

♥ Pay attention to how you talk to yourself and treat yourself. Overfunctioning can be a sign of low self-esteem.

♥ Develop several ways to nurture yourself. Make a list. For example:

  • *Take a break before you act.*
  • *Practice mindfulness (acting on purpose with fully focused attention.)*

- *Take a nap every day.*
- *Get a massage once a month.*
- *Stop and take three deep breaths.*

💜 Before you act, ask these questions:

- *What do I hope to get from this?*
- *Will this action give me the result I want?*
- *Is this my responsibility?*
- *Is this about helping my partner or helping myself?*
- *Am I doing this to manage my own feelings?*

Finally, for both partners: review the section on "Core Values" in Chapter 21. Individuals who have difficulty setting and respecting healthy personal boundaries often have an undefined sense of self. Core value living is one of the best ways to strengthen your personal sense of self and your self-esteem.

Once you determine your core values, write them down and keep them posted where you will see them frequently. At the end of each day you should be able to ask yourself: *How was I kind today? How was I supportive? How did I show self-respect?* The goal is to provide concrete examples of how your behavior each day reflects your own core values.

Lastly, remember that your strongest feelings are designed to bring you back to your core values. When your partner upsets you and when you disappoint yourself, use the reaction to take you directly to your core values. For example, if you feel anger, ask yourself: *What would a kind person do right now? What would a supportive person do right now? What would a person with self-respect do right now?* Use your core values to strengthen love and compassion for yourself as well as your partner.

20

Growing Apart Is Tearing Us Apart

How did we get to be such strangers? When did this void creep into our lives? Where is the energy and love? Why does every day feel so much like a chore? We aren't fun anymore. We aren't connected anymore. Sigh.

Somehow the life we've created, the life we used to love, has no room for us as a couple. You spend your time, I spend my time, but there is no "us time"—you know, those times when we used to enjoy being together. Now we are like two zombies just going through the motions of life.

Being close never used to be a question. We wouldn't let anything get in the way of our contact with each other. How did our lives become so full without making room for us? I know you are working hard and staying busy and everything you do is important, but our relationship seems lost in the past and you don't seem interested in getting it back. It's like we are roommates sealed off from each other with no interest in connecting again.

I know talking about this won't help; we've tried that time and again and it always drives us further apart. I don't have any answers, but there are questions that haunt me: Do you still love me? I mean do you really love me, desire me, long to be with me? Would you choose me as your partner again if you were starting over? Do you like our life? Would you leave me if you could? Have we become two people who no longer belong together?

The Purpose Behind Growing Apart

Few couples grow apart intentionally or consciously. In most cases, it sneaks up on you like a thief in the night. Couples don't realize how living essentially separate lives weakens connection and puts relationships at great risk of ruin.

Growing apart could easily be the greatest threat to relationships today, mostly due to unprecedented demands of the twenty-first century. Yes, you still find one another, fall in love, establish a relationship, and then go about the tasks of life just as it's been done for eons. However, it's the last part, going about the tasks of life, that most commonly causes relationships to dissolve.

Think about it. Work obligations extend into personal hours. Commuting to and from work takes time away. Children/family commitments absorb all the time you have if you let them. Add in time for religious activities, home repair and maintenance, not to mention keeping up with the cooking, cleaning, laundry, bill-paying, personal hygiene, shopping, and the list goes on . . . but we haven't even mentioned sleep, rest, recreation, hobbies, pastimes—or quality time for the relationship. *Whew!* Carving out time for the two of you can feel like one more obligation to fulfill. *If it's not an emergency, can't we just chill out instead?*

In some ways, it's easier to ignore a good relationship because it doesn't demand your attention. This is a common and unfortunate mistake. Unless someone is actively complaining, it's easy to take each other for granted while being responsible in other, albeit important, areas of life. The danger in this approach is that eventually you can get out of the habit of making time for each other, and all the other demands keep absorbing the time and energy the relationship needs in order to survive. In the process of being responsible you become irresponsible to the relationship.

Partners grow apart simply by following their individual interests. We all need outside interests to provide relief from work and renew our energy. Hobbies, pastimes, and recreation make us well-rounded and add spice to life. Most people pursue outside interests because they are enjoyable; rarely is the goal to get away from the partner or to take the first step toward growing apart. The problem for relationships is when personal interests are developed, but couple interests are not. There's trouble on the horizon when all the fun happens with other people, not the couple. This can happen by pure, innocent oversight; it can happen because you are thinking of yourself, kids, family members, friends, and not the relationship; it can happen by figuring your partner should be the one to invite you into the fun, not vice versa.

Lack of role models. One true sign of falling in love is prioritizing the relationship. When two people are infatuated they make time together a clear priority and feed the relationship with attention. Infatuated lovers remember details, listen to each other, come up with surprises, show affection, do romantic things, feel sensual and sexual, and they make one another feel special—they make each other a *priority*. The romantic high of infatuation can't go on forever at a fever pitch. Eventually, we have to go back to the demands of everyday life, and herein lies the problem.

Depending upon your relationship role models, you may not have a picture of what it looks like making the relationship a priority in everyday life. Your role model may have made the primary focus work, kids, or personal interests. You might just be going about your business, living life as you learned by your role models, but meanwhile you and your partner are growing apart.

Boredom. Some people find immense pleasure and comfort in routine. Doing the same activities day after day gives them a sense of security, constancy, and commitment. They do not find it dull, tedious, or monotonous. They find joy in a relationship that looks the same today as it did ten years ago. Then there are others for whom relationship routine is synonymous with death. Most of us fall somewhere in between these two extremes. Relationships can grow apart if the two of you don't find a way to establish a sense of security as well as novelty.

No effective way of managing differences. Couples who avoid conflict or manage conflict with abuse are at great risk for growing apart. If you don't have a way of not only managing but honoring differences, the relationship will die for lack of oxygen. Without the space to grow, change, and differ in opinions, two people will have to separate to survive. You may live together, you may go through the motions, but you will have to hide your true selves, and ultimately resentment will build a wall between the two of you. Some of the most polite, we-never-argue couples are seriously at risk of growing apart—and most don't even know it.

Partners who cannot effectively manage a difference of opinion often use anger, demands, blaming, controlling, forced agreement, micromanaging, passive-aggressive acts, and stonewalling—simply to cope with their own anxiety. An ineffective coping strategy may make you feel safe but ultimately will destroy the relationship.

No viable connection. Without ways and means to periodically connect, couples grow apart. Fortunately there are many ways to make a connection, but here are some common reasons why a person might not choose them.

- **Talking:** I can't talk to you because our conversations always end in a fight. You interrupt, correct, criticize, and always have to be right. I've given up trying to communicate with you this way.

- **Affection:** I can't even remember the last time you showed me any physical affection. When I reach out to you, I get the cold shoulder or I'm accused of only wanting sex.

- **Attention to Needs:** How can you expect me to be sensitive to your needs when you have ignored mine over and over again? I feel like a fool trying to please you when you seem to have no interest in pleasing me.

- **Sex:** When was the last time you initiated sex? Or even acted like you want to have sex? You've taken away the one activity that made us feel the most connected. How can you expect me to be helpful or romantic or even interested when you have shut me out sexually?

Or

- All you think about is sex. I'm just a sex object to you. If it weren't for sex would you be interested in me at all? Do you even like me? Want to spend time with me? How can I feel close to you when I feel so alienated by you sexualizing me?

- **Fun:** You won't join me in my idea of fun, and yet you don't have suggestions for other things to do.

Or

💜 How can you think about fun when we have so much to do? I don't get how you just ignore all the things that need to be done.

💜 **Joint Projects:** I know you have a "to-do" list for me, and if you were running my life I would spend all my spare time completing tasks. While I think some of this is important (mainly because you like it), that's not how I want to spend my spare time.

Even when you long for connection, when all avenues appear to be blocked, even the most loving partners can start growing apart.

The Disconnect from Growing Apart

Growing apart easily could be the most insidious issue for relationships because it creeps up on you and dangerously weakens the bond without conscious awareness. If you don't have consistent, positive ways of connecting, eventually you will grow apart. When two people have grown apart it's even easier for the relationship to be torn apart.

Growing apart creates a void not only in the relationship but also in the hearts of the two individuals involved. When your heart is empty, you are more vulnerable to outside sources of comfort, such as a friendly co-worker, a daily cocktail, a shopping spree, Internet porn, hobbies, gambling, love interests from the past, or being over-involved with children or friends.

When you've grown apart and your heart is empty, the disappointments in life have far more negative impact on you, and the relationship will suffer collateral damage. Rarely will two people split up just because they have grown apart, even though it is cited as the cause of breakups more often than any other. The true breakup comes from a breakdown in connection where a simple outside event merely represents the last nail in the relationship coffin.

The disconnect from growing apart is very powerful and dangerous for relationships. Couples must take the issue of growing apart seriously, even in its early stages.

Transforming the Growing Apart

There's good news and bad news when it comes to growing apart. The bad news is, it's very serious and can tear your relationship apart. The good news is, the way to fix it can be fun and highly rewarding.

Think of reconnecting the same way you save money: pay yourself first. Carve out time for your relationship and spend that time together even if it means cheating other aspects of your life. So what if you don't make the bed and you wear the same clothes you wore yesterday! Go to the bedroom and shut the door and tell the kids they can't come in unless there's an emergency involving fire, blood, or a broken bone. Put a date night on the calendar and attach a serious penalty for breaking it. Don't wait until you have time for each other; take time for each other and make other things wait!

- ❦ Do what works. Make a list of the activities you do together that always leave you in a better place with one another. If you don't know of any, make it a goal to discover the activities as a team.
- ❦ Get interested in each other's interests. You may not have liked bowling years ago, but times change and so do you.

💗 Reach out and touch each other. There's no substitute for the bonding effect of physical affection. Holding your partner's hand, touching the face, caressing the hair, and giving a shoulder massage can go a long way toward reconnecting the two of you.

💗 Jump-start your sex life. Focus on giving one another sensual and sexual pleasure.

💗 Focus on solutions instead of problems. Brainstorm ways to get reconnected again.

💗 Learn something new together.

💗 Make goals for your relationship and work on fulfilling them together.

If the two of you have grown apart to the point of being strangers, you may have to fight your way back—and one of you may have to carry the burden alone for a while. It's very powerful when even one person becomes energized on behalf of the relationship, especially in the face of opposition or apathy from the other partner. Follow your own core values and do your best to reconnect.

Be willing to make a drastic change in your lifestyle for the sake of your relationship. Many couples become trapped in the life they have created. The big home requires a big payment, which requires a big investment of time and energy. Big debts put big burdens on breadwinners. Financial pressure can take the joy out of life and sap all the energy from your relationship. Downsizing or right-sizing may be the only act that can save your relationship.

Get help—don't give in. Counselors, coaches, workshops, seminars, and retreats can help get you back on track, oftentimes more quickly than you can doing it alone.

21

Avoid the Wear and Tear— Shortcuts to a Great Relationship

S carlett O'Hara loved Rhett Butler but sure didn't act like it, and by the time she got through with him, he frankly didn't give a damn. For a long time Rhett had enough persistence for both of them, but despite beauty and charm, Scarlett's tantrums and manipulations—not to mention her whining and pining for Ashley—ultimately wore him out. While the romantics among us might have longed for a happy ending to this love story, anyone familiar with research would know that relationship was gone with the wind.

Research has clearly identified behaviors that tear couples apart, and little of the research surprises us. Studies show criticism, blame, defensiveness, withdrawal, and contempt do not bode well for relationships, and this makes sense. Couples who have far more negative than positive interactions break up more often—no surprise there.

It doesn't take Sigmund Freud to understand a woman who sees only her partner's shortcomings is more likely to leave, or a man who spends more time watching porn than participating in the relationship is likely to find himself alone. Simplistic insight, though, is not enough to make necessary changes; that's the reason we explored *why* a woman looks for shortcomings; *why* a man turns to porn; *what* tears a relationship apart; and *how* we prevent this from happening.

Years of clinical experience have taught us human behavior is complex, and we need to be compassionate about this complexity. There are, however, some fundamental practices that underlie *all* problems that threaten relationships, and if these practices are not in place, the connection between two people is weakened and more easily torn apart. So we end this book with good news: whether you are single or committed, if you want a shortcut to relationship happiness, these six strategies are for you!

Emotional Regulation

We list this practice first because emotional regulation easily can make or break a relationship. When one or both partners is unable to manage their emotions with maturity and consciousness, when feelings run rampant without consideration of their impact, then the relationship risks falling apart. Only when emotion is balanced with conscious thought and compassion will connection be restored and healing begin.

Emotion comes from the same root word as "to move," and emotional sensations tell us what to do in particular situations. When you have an experience your brain thinks is important, it marks it with emotion. Next time you're in a similar situation, you are motivated to respond in a particular manner based on that history. It is important to pay attention to emotions because they are designed to keep you safe—but feelings also can lead you astray. Your history may or may not accurately reflect what's going on in the present. If your former partner had an affair with a co-worker, you might get anxious every time your current partner works overtime. If your dad raged at you as a child, you may avoid conflict at any cost. Healthy relationships are based upon the ability to separate the past from the present and to make choices using rational thought as well as emotions.

Largely designed for protection, emotions are biased toward safety and tend to assume the worst. (In terms of survival it's safer to think a stick is a snake than a snake is a stick.) A neutral comment from your partner may be interpreted negatively so that you can be prepared to defend yourself. You can begin to see how those of us with a history of hurt, disappointment, abandonment, or abuse in relationships can get triggered very easily by the pain of the past. It's important to honor emotions, but many times it's just as vital to acknowledge the feeling—but make a *conscious* choice of how to act. Be certain that your emotions are not being reactivated from past experiences that are no longer relevant.

Taking personal responsibility for your own emotional well-being is part of maturity and mental health, and it's especially relevant in relationships. A love partner has the power to evoke strong feelings in us because so much is at stake. When you become attached to another person, whether it is emotional, psychological, physical, or legal, that individual takes on an enormous amount of importance in your psyche. Small issues become big issues when your partner's involved. (This explains why you become much more reactive and emotional when your partner is late than when an acquaintance is late. It also explains why a partner might say: "You are nicer to your friends than you are to me!")

The ability to calm yourself, regulate, and evaluate your own emotions is so important that it's next to impossible to be in a happy, stable, love relationship without it. When even one person is calm or rational, you cannot have an argument. You might have a heated discussion or you might have a vigorous debate—but it will not escalate without you both making it escalate. You cannot control how others manage their emotions, but you can learn to effectively manage your own. Regulating your emotions helps prevent tearing your relationship apart.

Core Value Living

When your daily life does not reflect your best self, your relationships will suffer. A lack of personal integrity will tear relationships apart, and core value living is the first step in putting them back together.

Right now, think of a person you hold in high regard. What is it about this person you admire? Is he loving? Is she supportive? Make a note of the characteristics that attract your attention. Next, ask yourself this question, "When I am dead and gone, how do I want the people I love most to remember me?" And finally ask yourself, "What kind of person do I want to be?" The answers to these questions will begin to reveal the character traits you admire and hope to emulate—your core values.

Personal standards should guide your everyday actions. If kind, loving, and supportive are your values, at the end of each day you should be able to ask yourself, "How was I kind? How was I loving? How was I supportive?" and get concrete answers: "I was kind when I came home early to cook dinner because Chris was not feeling well. I was loving when I returned Mom's call. I was supportive when I called Jordan about the test results."

The best relationships consist of two people living their core values. Being our best brings out the best in others. It doesn't guarantee it, but it greatly increases the chances of success. We are often asked, "Well, why should I be nice when my partner isn't nice?" Here's the answer: "Because you feel better about yourself when you do the right thing."

Doing the right thing means acting in a way that is congruent with your core values. Don't let your partner, or anyone for that matter, decide what kind of person you are going to be. You be your best, period. Core value living may not save every relationship, but it can prevent tearing them apart.

Compassion

Compassion is the desire to heal and not hurt. Compassion builds trust; trust leads to commitment; and commitment prevents coming apart.

Oftentimes compassion is confused with empathy, but it's far more. Empathy is simply feeling what another person feels, and while this is important and certainly a good first step, healthy relationships have to go beyond this. (Knowing what your partner feels can be used constructively or destructively. Think about it: just because I know what you are feeling doesn't mean I care or will act in a helpful manner; I can use that knowledge against you if I choose.)

This book asks you to go a step further than empathy because it's not enough simply to know *what* your partner is feeling. You also need to *care* what the feeling is and *desire* to ease any suffering. This is the difference between empathy and compassion. Empathy is knowing; compassion is caring. Empathy says, "I know how you feel." Compassion says, "I want to be part of the healing, not the hurting, so how can I help?" Caring people don't knowingly tear relationships apart.

Putting a Heart Around Yourself and Others

Putting a heart around a relationship issue means you make a choice to surround the problem with love and compassion, even when you don't feel like it or don't understand. The complexity of our emotions makes this a significant challenge. The way we make sense of our behaviors is to use our own internal logic. Others (especially your partner) may or may not understand your logic at the time. Putting a heart around it means you give the benefit of the doubt; you choose to stay in connection with your partner despite differences that may threaten to tear you apart.

Being in a relationship requires us to accept differences as well as imperfections. All relationships have challenges, and no one is perfect when it comes to meeting those challenges. Once you learn the transformation practices in this book, it's likely you won't implement them perfectly at first—because *knowing what* to do is very different than actually *doing it*. Essentially, that's why we need to cut ourselves some slack. Putting a heart around it is for those times when we all need a break.

An illustration from interpersonal neurobiology sheds light on the enormous complexity of behavior—it's all about connection and protection. Our brains are hardwired for connection. We depend on one another to help regulate our emotions and provide the care and contact necessary to survive as infants and thrive as adults. This hardwiring keeps us moving toward relationships.

At the same time, we're hardwired for protection. Part of your brain is always on alert for danger, surveying the environment for verbal and nonverbal signals—all in the service of keeping you safe. Sometimes these biological drives work in tandem, moving you toward relationships for contact, care, safety, and security. Other times they're at odds with one another, and the need to protect overrides the need to connect.

For example, if past experience taught your brain to associate a loud voice with violence or abuse, then your partner's loud voice might set off a protective alarm, even though your partner has never been violent or abusive. Your brain always interprets current events based upon past experiences. Therefore, your partner's loud voice signals a threat even when there is no present danger. These interpretations, as well as your responses, occur instantaneously without conscious thought or awareness. We are simply wired for habit.

The need to connect and the need to protect drive all human interaction. At any given time either or both can come into play. Sometimes these feelings are elegant and beautiful, and sometimes they literally can save your life. Other times these feelings can emerge shaped by fear from the past. Putting a heart around it is a reminder to look at all behavior with kindness, compassion, and understanding because there's much more going on than meets the eye.

Crossing the Bridge

The magic of true intimacy is the reward for having the courage to accept and love your partner as a separate person. Acknowledging the *otherness of the other* is a prerequisite for connection. Anything short of this will not bring the joy we all long for.

So how do you begin to enter your partner's world when that world is different than yours? You start by crossing the bridge of separation. The mirror neuron system in your brain makes crossing the bridge possible by enabling you to follow and understand each other's movements, behaviors, and emotions. You cross the bridge from your world into your partner's world by acknowledging that both worlds exist. You visit one another's reality without denying your own.

Some partners learn to cross the bridge by curiosity: What is it like for you when I withhold sex? When I criticize you, what goes on inside your head? How does it make you feel when I spend longer and longer hours at work? When I'm nicer to my friends and co-workers than I am to you, what does that do to our relationship? Others learn to cross the bridge by visualizing two worlds connected by a bridge of love.

Learning to cross the bridge means you are able to manage your emotions, hold on to your core values, experience your partner's world with compassion, and put a heart around your differences. All this requires a great deal of maturity, and perhaps that's why the payoff is so big. There is a definite WOW! factor when two souls meet and cross the bridge into relationship. It's what lovers rave about in the throes of infatuation.

When you cross the bridge of separation into the world of the other, you become linked by the experience of connection. This connection occurs when you hold on to your unique self, while simultaneously seeking to acknowledge and understand your partner's reality. Couples long for these magic moments of connection.

Integration

If I expect you to be exactly like me, then there's only one
of us—and that's one person short of a relationship.

A powerful shortcut to healthy relationships is the ability to hold on to your individuality while staying connected and tuned in to one another. This integration begins by learning to embrace your partner's differences with curiosity, objectivity, and compassion. It's one thing to cross the bridge and acknowledge the separate reality of your partner, but it's another to honor, respect, and truly embrace your differences.

As individuals, we are one-of-a-kind—we are *different*. We come equipped with our own set of genes that distinguish us from others. Our genetic makeup is then shaped by experiences, which further define our uniqueness. We express our individuality through our behavior, beliefs, and interpretation of the world around us.

A relationship consists of two separate individuals who are joined by love. The same differences that draw you together in the beginning often become a source of unhappiness and disconnect later on. Your differences likewise cause you to see the world differently. Many relationship struggles emerge from the belief that there is only one reality—*mine*. In other words, "It's my way or the highway!"

Differentiation requires you to be your own person in the presence of your partner and to honor your partner's uniqueness. This takes courage, especially when differences cause anxiety for either of you. A healthy relationship has the resilience to hold your deepest connections and individual differences through a process known as integration.

Without integration, passion will wane and romance will turn routine at best and nonexistent at worst. When partners honor the ever-changing aspects of each other's personalities, you will create an unlimited source of energy and excitement.

Integration involves bringing together two separate individuals, and as a result, sometimes we need to go apart so that we can be together. This may sound strange and even tricky, but it has a logical explanation. It takes two people to make a relationship; it takes two people to feel the joy of connection; it takes two people to keep passion alive; and it takes two people to sustain a relationship, even though it only takes one to tear it apart.

- ♥ If you say you love me, but you don't know me, how can that be true?
- ♥ If you say you love me, but don't acknowledge my separate reality, how can that be true?
- ♥ If you only love me when I think and act like you, isn't that really loving you and not me?

You will never feel the magic of connection if the requirement is for both of you to be just alike or to stay the same as the day you met. Connection only happens between two separate, distinct, and ever-evolving individuals. You will never feel completely understood if you give up your authentic self to be accepted by your partner. Resentment will thrive in any relationship where you can't be honest about who you are.

The magic in relationships grows from acknowledging and loving your true selves and integrating your differences.

These half-dozen practices—emotional regulation, core value living, compassion, putting a heart around it, crossing the bridge, and integration—will form a protective perimeter around your relationship. The concepts are not complicated, yet every relationship that's torn apart begins with a violation of one or more of these six practices.